HEALING THE HEART

by

Rodger Christopherson

<u>Other books by the author</u>

A Little Bit of Anarchy
Out of the Fire Mist
Monkey in a Tree
After the President Disappeared
Three Weeks Until Tomorrow
Illusions
Health - non fiction
Beyond Science & Religion - non fiction
How Science & Religion Have Failed Humanity - non fiction
Circles in the Sand - Poetry

Comments and questions---

  intercept777@centurylink.net

BAD NEWS

The cardiologist's office was a block off Wilshire Boulevard, just a short distance from Cedars Sinai Hospital in Beverly Hills and my first time there even though I had now known the man for about two years.

"I'd like to go to Peru," I told him. "Do you think it would be okay? The altitude?"

"Well," he said, and pondered for a moment. "Take your shirt off and sit up on the table."

I did. The stethoscope was cold. He moved it around on my bare chest and listened. Then he nodded and I put my shirt back on, waiting for him to say I was fit to go. But he didn't.

"I think we should do one more test," he said instead. "Just to be sure."

Reluctantly I said okay and asked what it was.

"A stress thallium."

"What's that?"

He explained it briefly.

"How much is that going to cost?" Me, with no insurance.

"Twelve hundred dollars."

I winced.

"Just to be safe," he said. "Then I can give you a clear answer."

Well, hell, I wondered. Was this another one of those medical, cover your ass tests or did he really suspect something? Then I back tracked. Why would I even begin to question him. Two years earlier this doctor had taken a personal risk and saved my life in the process. I shrugged and nodded my approval. He picked up the phone, dialed, spoke, listened, wrote something on his prescription pad and handed it to me. It contained the name and address of a private imaging company. Thursday afternoon, one o'clock.

"Make an appointment with my secretary to come back here on Friday. I'll have the results by then. Okay?"

"Sure. Thank you."

Shirtless again, but now with at least a dozen electrode pads pasted on my upper body, front and back, I looked at the super sized syringe full of a greenish liquid laying on the stand beside the treadmill and the already implanted catheter in my arm just above my wrist. What had I committed my self to?

"All right," the technician said. "Up on the treadmill. Now hang on to the supports. Okay, now I'm going to run the speed up slowly. In three or four minutes I'll stop so we can inject you, Then you'll have to run again until we get you heart rate up to at least one twenty. Ready?"

Not really, I thought. Me, by now feeling more like an impersonal object than a human being. But that was what I was there for so I nodded my head and the belt under my feet began to move. Not liking it one bit, however, I was still able to keep pace with the machine and that portion of the procedure was soon over. The belt stopped. One person held my arm, the other inserted the monstrous syringe into the catheter and began the injection. It burned as it went in. Hell yes. Why shouldn't it? It was radioactive. Then the belt was moving again under my feet, but this time it was different. Impossibly different.

It was going faster for one thing. And the angle of incline was also increased. I was now being forced to run up hill, me pitted against the machine. But why did my feet feel so heavy? Why did it seem like such hard work? I didn't understand. Was I that far out of condition, I wondered as I struggled to keep up.

"I can't do this," I finally told the tech as he looked at the numbers on the panel.

He shook his head. "Keep going. We're not even close

4

yet."

I tried. I really tried as the belt speed increased but things began to hurt, particularly my chest. Finally unable to continue, I yelled for him to stop, the test be damned.

"Your pulse isn't even up to ninety yet," he stated as he slowed, then stopped the machine. "You need to try it again."

"I don't care, I can't do this. I think you're trying to kill me."

He didn't respond to that but consulted with the older man who had now came over and looked at the monitors instead. Then, given some kind of instruction, he helped me off the treadmill, removed all the electrode pads and wires from my body and told me to follow, no explanation given.

In an adjacent room I was told to get up onto a long, pad less, very cold metal table. I obeyed. Over head was a rather large, movable sensor head that, once programed, would rotate in a large arc around my upper body and record the particles emanating from the radioactive thallium which by now had to be passing through my heart. Hopefully enough so live images could be formed as it pumped away.

"Try to lie still," the technician stated as he made some adjustments, still being as impersonal as before. Then he punched the go button and abruptly walked out of the room.

Lay still, hell. The room might be comfortable for someone working but as for me, shirtless, lying on this cold platform? I began to shiver.

"Anyone here," I asked, unable to see and not wanting to move even my head. Nothing, except that I was freezing. What seemed like an hour went by before the tech finally came back.

"I'm cold. Can I have a blanket?"

No response.

He checked the control panel instead as the sensor head moved a few more degrees around the circle, then left the room and came back with a thin blanket which he put over me, turned and left again, no words spoken. Better. Slightly. At least I stopped shivering and I shut my eyes, trying to blank out the entire experience from my mind. Something I had gotten considerably better at the last few years. Finally the machine stopped making noises and came to a halt. The agony was over. The technician watched as I got off the table, gave me my shirt, checked my mailing address to make sure as to where to send the bill and I was free to go.

And then it was Friday.

The doctor was sitting behind his desk when I came into his office and waved me into the chair in front. Once seated, he looked at me.

"How are you you feeling," he asked politely enough, not giving anything away.

"I don't know. Decent enough, I guess," I said, hoping for some good news. But let him tell me. He was the expert, the cardiologist, the decider.

He scrutinized my face carefully before he spoke. It wasn't an authoritative voice. Nor did it seem particularly concerned. Or sympathetic. Just a voice speaking the truth as he saw it.

"Well," he said after a brief pause and handed me a new prescription that doubled the dosage of my medication. "Seriously, if I were you, I wouldn't go anywhere that wasn't across the street from a good hospital. You could drop over any minute."

LOST

Had I been given a death sentence? It certainly seemed so. How ironic. Now I was sitting on death row in my own private prison of events because I had spent the last two years doing what I had been told to do and this is how it ended up anyway. Fruit, fish and fowl as a diet, moderate exercise, no smoking, keep the weight down, get plenty of rest and above all, take the prescription meds as specified. So, having done this faithfully and still ending up with such a depressing end result, how was I ever to get well? It seemed obvious that I probably wasn't going to. At the time, however, this was not a well thought out conclusion, it was a sub verbal realization instead, perhaps left there on purpose because of all the depressing implications. So what was I to do when there seemed to be nothing that could be done? That was the unanswerable question I was burdened with at the time. And who to tell? Certainly not my three adult children. If I was going to die, let it be a surprise, not something for them to spend time worrying about ahead of time. As for my wife, she was now the ex-wife I no longer mattered to. And then there was Sharon, the woman I was living with at the time of the initial heart attack but that relationship was now long over so where did that leave me? I drove home and tried not to think about it.

The next morning, my mind shut down as I threw a few clothes into some travel bags, put them in my car and started driving. To where? I had no idea and so, completely arbitrary, I started going east out of Los Angeles. Highway 10. Riverside, Palm Springs, Indio and eventually Blythe, all left behind as I crossed the Colorado River into Arizona, soon to be greeted by an immense array of Saguaro Cactus standing out in the sand with their arms up, as if in greeting. Another twelve miles further, the sign said Quartsite, but no point in stopping there.

Then, another ten miles, a two lane road leading off to the left. Automatically I got off the freeway and headed north, first stop, Salome.

Salome, population, not many. Out in the desert. A bar, a couple of motels, some RV parks for the snow birds, a few small stores. I stopped at the bar and had a sandwich, still ignoring my feelings. Then, back in the car, more desert as I passed through the tiny towns of Wendon and Aguila and took the next road left that led to Congress and on up the mountain to Yarnell, through Peeples Valley and Wilhoit into the pine tree forest and on to Prescott. It was around four o'clock in the afternoon and I stopped at the very first motel coming into town. I had to. The altitude was only five thousand feet but I knew I was in trouble. I was beginning to feel a certain painful tightness in my chest. And I was exhausted. I checked into the motel, went straight to my room and crawled into bed.

Why hadn't I suspected something was wrong before, I wondered the next morning, back in my car, heading thru this old western town, now on the road to Jerome? Somehow that stress thallium test seemed to have precipitated a physically very unpleasant, unwanted condition in my body. Something that damn well might kill me before I ever got to wherever I was going, where ever that might be, as yet unclear and never existed when I first started out. But, okay, and by the time I was finished with that round of thought I was through town and out into the Prescott Valley, a time long before the freeway, all the tract houses and commercial development. First, a two lane road that went through Granite Dells with boulders bigger than houses and then out into a large, high mountain meadow full of wildflowers. Miles of wildflowers. Blues and yellows, orange and purple all smiling in the sun. I stopped the car and got out to enjoy it more fully. But as I did, an immense sadness swept over

8

me instead and tears came to my eyes. So much left undone, unvisited, unseen, so many things now out of reach. Where was I going, what was I going to do when I got there, if I ever did? Truly lost, thinking only of myself, it all seemed so unfair.

Moving on, the road wound its way upward, back into the forest, then switch-backed its way down into the old mining town of Jerome clinging to the side of the mountain. And then the realization that almost caused an accident. We had been this way before. But going in the opposite direction, coming home from the Midwest to California twenty four or twenty five years earlier. Three little kids in the back of our new station wagon, probably four, five and six at the time, standing up, looking out the windows. And beside me in the front, their mother, my wife, the victim of melanoma, gone at thirty one. More deep sadness, something else still unresolved.

But at last, safely down the mountain and through the largely unremembered town of Cottonwood, on the left side of the road, still only two lanes wide back then, a wall of red rocks, brilliant with the sun angle just right. A little further, more red rocks, and up the hill and around the corner, the town of Sedona, still relatively small, with an immensity of red rock formations laid out against its backdrop of high mountains. No point in trying to describe it further. Words alone would be an injustice. It should have been a National Park instead, to protect the beauty from all the greed and stupidity that was to follow. But it didn't stop me from driving. Oak Creek Canyon, part way up Schnebly hill, out to the Village of Oak Creek, this street, that back road and, before I knew it, it was late afternoon and I was beginning to fade. Nothing like the day before, however, but still an alarming discomfort so I back tracked to a sign I had seen earlier. Sky Ranch Lodge. It was a motel up on top of airport mesa. I went there, checked in and again went directly to bed.

When I woke it was dark outside. The clock said eight fifteen. Now what? I laid there and the more awake I became, the more depressed and lonely I felt. Then, and I remember it clearly, even after all these years. Then I said to myself, well, I could lay there on that damned bed and die, or, I could get up, go somewhere, have dinner and try to make something out of the rest of my life.

About a mile down the street from the airport road in west Sedona was an upscale restaurant and nightclub hidden back in the trees. I parked, went it and ordered the most expensive item on the menu. That done and over with, I went into the bar room. One couple sitting at a table in the open area, and one woman at the bar talking to the bartender. I went past her and sat on a stool a little further down. I ordered a draft beer, got it and sipped it as the woman began talking to the bartender again. What was that? She was talking about Ethiopia. That sounded interesting, to me at least. Maybe not so much to the bartender because he seemed relieved when the couple at the table waved him over. With perfect timing I took the opportunity to ask if she had been there. She had, and was more than willing to share her story. Moving next to her, she talked, we talked. More beer and more talk. Not only had she been to Ethiopia, she had gone alone and back packed her way through the country, even sleeping on the ground in the villages with the natives around the fire. Then she moved on up into Egypt, worked her way across, took a boat over to Greece, did the same thing and then came home because she was out of money. Now she was working in a real estate office, saving money so she could go back to college.

Impressed, hell. I was overwhelmed. Mary Kay. At

least ten years younger than I, five foot five, medium build, how brave can one person get? And did I like to hike, she asked. Sedona is a fabulous place to go hiking and she would go with me if she didn't have to work the next day. But, as a starter, why didn't I go up to West Fork?

What? Me? I said to myself. Out in the woods a long ways from across the street from a hospital? It was ridiculous but I nodded anyway and asked for her phone number. But instead of giving me one, she agreed to meet at a restaurant in the uptown area the next evening.

The following morning, disregarding the Doctor's advice and everything logical, I drove up the canyon to the mile marker she had given me, parked, crossed the road, found the trail head and began to walk. Rock walls, tall trees, water tumbling over boulders. I had been living in the big city far too long, that was for sure. The trail inclined upward, but only slightly. It should have been easy. But, it was not. After what might have been half a city block, I stopped, leaned against a tree and put a nitro pill under my tongue. After the pain eased and I caught my breath, I did it again. Stupid, probably risking my life at this higher altitude, I was still determined to be able to say I had hiked that trail. I walked slower on the next lap and made it a little further. More rest, another nitro, go a little further. Half a mile, I guess, before I turned back. But it was an immense accomplishment. Additionally, flirting with death had at least made it more clear that I was still alive and reawakened the desire to stay that way.

A very long nap in the afternoon and there was Mary Kay, right where she said she would be. Dinner, a stroll through the uptown area, another bar and some beer. And a lot more conversation. Later we went up to my motel where my room looked out over the town below and sat outside until it was quite late. Then I drove her home.

Home was her sister's house out in the village. She was house sitting for the time being but never told me where she really lived. I walked her to the door where we hugged and it seemed as if she didn't want to part. But everything seemed okay after we agreed to meet again the following night. Friday night.

The evening was somewhat of a repeat except that she didn't have to work the next day so after eating and a few drinks, we came back to my motel where she spent the night. And the next one. Softness and sweetness that warmed my body and my spirit. It looked like I wasn't going to drop over dead just yet after all. So, since she had to go back to work on Monday I decided to go back home myself. There were things that needed to be attended to. But I would be back? Damn right. I knew that for sure because this seemed to be the undefined destination I had unknowingly set out for earlier in the week. And I was.

Three more times that summer. Twice for a week and once almost two weeks. We explored, we took short hikes and we talked and talked. Always something new to talk about and to learn and the second time there, she told me the truth. Except for the week she stayed in her sister's house, she had been living alone in a tent out in the forest south of town. Why? Primarily to save the most money possible so she could go back to school. Not so bad, she said. And it came with certain freedoms. Like walking around naked in the moon light. That I would have liked to see, I told her. But no, she said. When I was in town she would rather sleep in a bed than on the ground and have someone to snuggle up to.

Never once did I tell her about my condition, however. I didn't want to because I would have found it to be very embarrassing because I felt limited and weak. Additionally, I wanted nothing better than to ignore the truth about my health and my questionable future. And then suddenly it was fall and she was off to Flagstaff, going to college. I went there once to meet her, could see she was on a path that excited her, so we had lunch, spent some time in the tiny little house together that she had rented and said goodbye. But, after having gone only a few yards, I came back, gave her an immensely long hug, told her that I loved her and walked off. Up to this point in my life she had been the best therapy I had ever had, physically and emotionally and even though she didn't know it, I owed her tremendously. As for pursuing her further, it wouldn't have been fair. She had a new life, I had yet to put mine back together, if indeed I was to have one.

EARLIER

If I had to pick a point as to where the chain of events which led to this unfortunate mid-life outcome probably began, I would say it was ten years earlier. Somehow my second wife and I negotiated a divorce. It was complicated, delicate and a bit sad. Sad for her because it wasn't what she really wanted. Sad for me because I could think of no other way to resolve our differences. Thirteen years of knowing each other and eleven years of marriage that started out well enough. She was younger, attractive, very intelligent, adventuresome, and a great cook. We lived together in California, Minnesota, Maryland and back in California. We had nice houses, new cars and all the amenities that made for a decent middle class life. I came with three young children whose mother had died and needed someone to take her place and she came with one from her previous marriage who needed a father. But that wasn't all. She also came with some deep childhood wounds that only surfaced after we were wed and slowly evolved into something much worse. Emotionally disturbed, increasingly alcoholic, sometimes suicidal, without warning, things would erupt into dramatic chaos with children caught in the crossfire.

It wasn't that she was unhappy with me or the children. She was at war with herself and when that battle raged there was little to be done except to make sure she didn't do something self inflicted. It was a burdensome situation that I had no idea of how to deal with at the time. She thought we needed marriage counseling, I thought she needed a therapist to deal with some deeper issues first but she refused to go alone. Still, in the end she was very gracious about the situation, never once blamed me for any of it and agreed to an amicable divorce. Once that was done, she found an apartment and took her son with her. I was left with the house until it could be sold. No children for me. They were now adults living elsewhere. As for our relationship apart. In many respects it flourished and physically, it was back to what it had been before we had gotten married. Additionally, since we both understood that we would never reconcile, we were both very helpful to each other in transitioning back into the singles world. I supported her in new relationships and she found a couple of women she thought I might like to go out with. Then she met a man she began spending a lot of time with and I become a member of a private singles organization.

Dinner parties and dancing, almost all of which were on the right side of the hill, over in the more affluent areas of west Los Angeles in the very nice houses of women who obviously had well to do ex husbands. There were also monthly parties at the Marina in the penthouse of the organizations founder. The perfect situation at the time. I wasn't looking for a replacement wife. No thanks. I just wanted to expand my horizons and have a good time.

Of course I met a lot of interesting women but only a few became especially significant. Others were simply dating experiences, the how of which I had to completely relearn, and a few were important because they lead me to someone else. So, this being the case, one woman led me to her friend, a major songwriter of the times. But her career wasn't the important part. What was important was the almost ready made, instant connection between us. And, what was really good about her was that she had this wild, raucous sense of humor, was extremely out going and verbal, seemed to have adored me and expressed it often. After my failed marriage and some forced career changes, it was exactly what I needed at the time, whether she really meant it or not. She also literally had dozens and dozens of friends and knew a lot of people I had only read about but finally got to meet, which led in still more directions.

Another helpful person was an older southern woman. Never a mentor, a muse or a companion, she sponsored my membership into a charity that was heavy with singles and many recognizable people from the entertainment world and it was uplifting to be associated with them at various organizational functions.

Then there was a woman from Canada I used to visit and occasionally travel with and finally, after nearly three years of playing the singles game, this younger woman came up to me at a party.

Standing close in, she said, "Hi, there. Would you like to dance?"

"Of course," I answered, checking her out, not very sure as to why I might want to do that. Not that I didn't like aggressive women. I did because it was always clear up front what they did or did not want and avoided a lot of pretentious game playing and frivolity while trying to get to knowing them. That said, two dances later she, Sharon, gave me her phone number. Still uncertain as to what might come of it, however, I called her two days later. Our first date was a long walk on Venice beach and an evening in her hot tub with two bottles of champagne. The next was a long weekend together in Morro Bay, up the California coast. And with that I gave up a trip to Tahiti with another singles group that was going island hopping on sailboats to be able to see her. And with one exception when she was gone on a trip to Europe for a week, I soon found myself spending a lot more nights at her house than I did in the apartment I now lived in on her side of the hill. Shortly after that I also gave up the apartment, stored my furniture in the garage she never used out back and we were a couple living together. It was in September. The end of summer, and it was then, one night at dinner that she asked me if I had a tuxedo.

"No but I can always rent one."

"It would be better if you bought one instead. You'll be needing it."

"Okay. I can do that."

"Get it by Friday. We're going to a black tie event."

It was a charity ball, one of several that her company supported. This was done by purchasing very expensive seats at tables for the event. Dinner, entertainment and dancing. But in her case the company did not just buy two tickets, it paid for a whole table of ten. Furthermore, not only was she was the one who actually handled these things in the company's name but was also the one who decided who got to sit at that table. Usually it was company executives who needed a perk but sometimes included other business or political persons the company wished to cultivate. Up to that point in the relationship the one thing we rarely ever talked about was our jobs, except to acknowledge that we both had one and it was then that I began to realize that she probably earned a lot more than I did. I was simply the head of the engineering department of a hi tech company but she reported directly to the CEO of a top ten corporation. But then, bottom line, so what!

What was also unusual about our relationship was that it seldom, if ever, touched on the past except in those rare instances when it impacted the present. And in that regard, when we finally separated, it ended with me actually knowing very little about the details of her background. Still enough, however, for me to realize that the only thing that really mattered was that it led her to the party where we had met. Of course she had had other relationships, but with who and for how long I never knew nor cared. It did come as a surprise, however, what role she played in the major event and party season and broadened my perspective of what happened in the city.

Except for at least ten million too many people that overcrowd and overburden, the extended LA area still had a lot going for it as far I was personally concerned. Sandy beaches, cool ocean breezes, the movie industry, art galleries and museums, cultural diversity and an occasional earthquake to remind people that some things are still beyond their control. As for the people who attended black tie affairs, wearing a sequined gown or a tuxedo never made them anything more than they already were, in any way whatsoever.

While not a totally new experience for me, this aspect of the social scene was still one seen from a different perspective when being with Sharon. As for her, she had been doing this for several years and privately admitted that it was getting to be tedious. Not so much the actual events but some of the people that attended them. Snobbery, over jeweled pretense, self aggrandizement. The same characteristics displayed by people most everywhere except that here she was the one who had to deal with many of them personally, something she was actually very good at but nonetheless, I quickly began to see her point. Regardless, once everyone took their seats and dinner was served, they were still enjoyable events we liked going to.

All of these parties, however, turned out to be rather ordinary by comparison when contrasted with one major annual event. That was the birthday party of the company CEO, Sharon's boss which was noted for the extreme in extravagance. This party, thanks to Sharon and her staff, brought four or five hundred people together from as far away as Europe and the far east, each with some purpose behind it. Bottom line, if there wasn't something to be gained from a person's being there, they weren't there. The guest list included religious leaders, the head of a movie studio, a few movie stars just for show, company presidents, upcoming people of interest in the technology field and key members on the company board of directors. As for the after dinner speech making, what else would it be but full of flattery and conciliation. And a little over the top as shown by a well known but pretentious religious leader who said, "This is the kind of birthday party God would give for himself. If he could afford it."

Highly orchestrated as it was, it made each yearly party quite impressive. Five course meals, four kinds of wine on the tables, the entire Los Angeles Chamber Music orchestra playing in the background. Later, Dom Perignon, birthday cake, celebrity vocalists and instrumentalists

Regardless, what I enjoyed the most was the chance to watch the people. In particular, I liked observing couples, trying to assess what their relationships might be like in comparison to our own. Take the president of the corporate entity which Sharon's boss was the CEO of, and his wife. At one birthday party I couldn't help but see how they related because, mostly they didn't. During dinner, dessert and afterward he actually only spoke to her twice, very briefly. Otherwise he was fully occupied talking to other men at their table. Too bad he couldn't have seen the bigger truth. The eyes tell it all. Her's told me that she was lonely and bored. And perhaps ready to over step the bounds of marriage. Maybe already had and was willing to do it again. And then there was Sharon and I. Much more different than that, we had our own set of problems.

Beginning a relationship is easy. Sustaining one is a great deal harder. Ours lasted almost five years. It began with a passion that persisted right to the end. That part of it never changed. Actually, I guess, fundamentally, nothing changed and that was the real problem. In the meantime we had dinner out several nights a week, went to art gallery openings and the movies, lectures and meetings and made many three or four day trips down to Mexico. There we often stayed in out of the way small towns where we loved to walk around in the evening and enjoy the people, eat in local restaurants or simply sample the hot delicacies push cart vendors served. We also stayed in upscale resorts, preferring those along the coast and on the water. In other words, we had a rather interesting, very busy life together.

"It's all just so damned comfortable," she said once, one Sunday morning after nearly five years of being together when we were sitting outside having breakfast. Yes, it was comfortable. Very comfortable, when expressed in the way she meant it. If only she had said something just a little different, I often thought later. But she had not and at the same time, what was wrong with me that I wasn't able to explain what I needed in a way that she might have better understood and responded to? I couldn't, simply because, at the time, I didn't know how. And of all the things that had happened and were happening, that is what I struggled with most. The reason seemed to be that I didn't know how because I never learned how. At least that is what I say when looking for something to blame it on.

To a large extent, I think much of it was a generational thing. A different time, long before modern conveniences, life was often very harsh, especially in the rural areas struggling with the land. Life and death on the farm for my ancestors and family. And then the depression and the war. People didn't talk about their feelings. Things were tough enough without starting down that road. And maybe it was best to keep the ones you loved the most at the greatest arm's length away, otherwise how would you ever be able to deal with it if something serious should happen to them? It was what people did. Day by day, it was how they got through their life. And, unfortunately it was the way both Sharon and I had personally learned to cope and were trying to cope, her with some earlier tragedy and me with my own. Hers, she kept locked away behind many layers of repression and denial while mine kept bubbling up, getting in the way, creating confusion,disparity and dissatisfaction until in the end, I had to leave her. Everything else be damned, driven by earlier loss and a recent near death experience, there was no other way. The personal immensity of that previous loss was never fully realized , however, until after the divorce from from my second wife was over.

It began with the day when I woke up and realized there was no one in the bed beside me and the house was far too quiet. Breakfast alone was bad enough but the empty house in the evening put me in complete despair. I hadn't thought it would be that way at all. I would have my freedom, I could throw a few parties, have a new life. But with whom? Outside of my job I really knew very few people. Still, given time, I told myself, I could meet new people and make new friends, but in the meantime, what? Nothing, it seemed because it was really about something else entirely. Something from even further back in the past.

Back then, in the evening after the day was done, our three little children would cuddle close around their mother, my first wife, on the couch as she read bedtime stories before tucking them in with hugs and kisses. It was an everlasting, perfect picture. They were five, six and seven at the time. Less than a year later, however, they were motherless.

Melanoma, stated the doctor, and carved a hand sized amount of flesh off her back which included the tiny lump that had suddenly appeared there. But it was already too late. Its heedless growth had encompassed a blood vessel and passed malignant cells into the blood stream where they found their way throughout the body. Lumpectomy after lumpectomy, chemotherapy, pulsed laser radiation, x-rays, I don't think she wanted any of it but subjected herself to it out of response to the desperation felt by those around her. Then, one day my oldest daughter, then eight, called me at work. "Mommy fell down and can't get up," she said.

Even in the hospital, totally without complaint, she did her best to smile and cheer those who came to see her. The dreadful pain, impossible as it must have been near the end, was never too much and she was alert and in control, accepting of her fate, always graceful but of all things, I sure as hell didn't want her to die. And for nearly three months straight, I went to see her every night in the hospital.

Finally, however, less than eight months from the initial onset, only thirty one years old, at four in the morning, she slipped away. By the time I left the hospital the sky was graying in the east. Lost, I went into a nearby coffee shop and sat down. Customers came and went, cars moved in the street, people went to work, the sun came up just as it had the day before, the rest of the world was unconcerned and unaware. It was dreadful, confusing and impossible to understand, made even more so by what had happened previously.

Three months earlier there was a bright young secretary at work who always seemed to know everyone's birth date and baked a special cake for the occasion. She drove an old car she could barely afford and the men would help her with repairs to keep it running. At break time she would often come into my office, sit on the desk and tell me about her boyfriends, her life, the girlfriend she shared an apartment with. Then, one day her roommate's father evicted her sixteen year old brother from the house and he moved into the apartment with the two girls. On the weekend she baked another birthday cake for someone at work and the brother purposely ruined it with his fingers. In trying to stop him he went into a rage and brutally murdered her with a kitchen knife. She was only twenty two. Then, within less than a year of the others, my best friend died of heart failure, also at far too young an age. They were all exceptional people. Kind, caring, generous, involved, self sufficient and necessary.

Shortly after my wife's funeral the minister of the church she occasionally attended, stopped by in a fumbled attempt to console but spent most of his time pathetically expressing his personal fear about the small, benign growth that had been removed from his own neck. Even the surgeon himself, the one who had carved away on my wife so desperately all those months, told me of his own deeper concern. He was going to have his partner remove a small mole on his own cheek, too. Then, a few days after the funeral some stranger had clipped the obituary notice out of the paper, laminated it in plastic and sent it to me in the mail along with an inane Biblical quote and a request for twenty dollars. And for weeks after that it was shallow condolences of "God works in mysterious ways" and other trite attempts to provide consolation which were totally incapable of giving even the smallest bit of necessary comfort. Even worse, in spite of assuming they were all put forth with good intent, in that lost and desperate time where neither modern medicine or religion was able to extend her life, they came across as stupid, superficial and meaningless, as indeed they were.

And, so what, some may say. Look at what else is going on in the world. War and genocide. Millions of innocent people caught up in the havoc, maimed and slaughtered simply because they were in the wrong place at the wrong time. Nothing more, just victims of other people's madness. What about them? Where is justice when so often there is not one single family member or friend left alive to even mourn them? Tough questions for sure, questions that often make life seem even more meaningless than it already appears to be, especially when personal tragedy strikes.

Then too, on the other side of it, what I was supposed to tell my children? That somehow their mother's death was "God's will?" Was that supposed to make it all right? How could it? For me, simply dumping the blame on God was much too irresponsible and unsatisfying. I loved and respected my children more than that. Regardless of the proportions of our personal situation, however, their world and mine had changed irrevocably. And even though rational answers appeared to be unavailable, my sanity still demanded more.

It was not to be found, however. Not then, anyway. Additionally, I could find no one capable of helping me deal with it and I think family and friends were by far the worst. Maybe they thought it wasn't the right thing to do. Or perhaps it was just too painful for them but their refusal to talk about this person they also once knew felt like cruelty to me and almost literally, sometimes made me question my own sanity. I had known her for thirteen years. We had lived together for twelve, had three bright, beautiful children and, good intentions be damned, almost everyone was denying her and her existence, and that hurt badly.

As for the marriage itself, it was exceptional. Like many, we started out poor and hopeful and worked our way up. At the end we lived in a lovely house on an old tree lined street where she said she would like to stay until our children were all through school. I fully agreed. It was like almost everything else between us. We never fought. There were no harsh words. Whatever happened, we faced it together and things just worked themselves out. But even so some guilt remains, will always remain, justified or not, that's just the way it is. How many times could I have held her closer and hugged her more and told her how lovely she was? Of all things, she deserved that the most. And then, looking back, all those other the lingering questions. What if? What if she had lived? How then would it have all played out? Most certainly my children would have been far better off. I saw that when they were growing up without her. I see it now when I am around them, thinking how much richer their lives might have been with her there, supporting them and cheering them on.

And what about the rest of it. Could I have gone on being the kind of husband she deserved? Me, the person who never thought they ever wanted to get married in the first place. And me, the person who looked at other people's children and never wanted any of my own but ended up with three I absolutely loved and adored. The person who, alone, would never be able to make up for the loss they encountered. And what about my own career aspirations with my personal value system turned upside down? What indeed was more important than what now?

The memories of that beautiful person and the questions that arose from her death at such a young age never went completely away, even though the many years passed. Questions, always, as my mind reached out in search of some larger explanation for it all. Questions which for many years I was not capable of asking clearly because, at the time, all I was capable of doing was maintaining. Regardless of all else, I still had a job I couldn't do without and three small children who still needed parenting, now more then ever, and that's the way it was. Getting them off to school in the morning, going back to work, doing the shopping and the laundry, taking them out for a hamburger, going to the park, making it through the day. And then, at night after the baby sitter arrived and they were in bed, my own diversions. Running, running, running. Bar hopping, dating other women, staying out late, wearing myself out, determined to survive one way or another, keeping what remained of my life together. And that is essentially what led me to getting married to my second wife.

Unfortunately, that marriage, with all of its problems, led to the divorce. And then the real difficulty began. It wasn't parting with my ex wife. For the most part, I welcomed that. It was what it triggered instead. It was all those years of staying too busy to have effectively dealt with the loss of my first wife. Side stepping it, pushing it away, avoiding dealing with it at all costs. But then, suddenly, there I was. Just me alone in an empty house once again and the past came flooding in. Not only did it come flooding in, it very nearly washed me away. And while I may have done a good job of hiding my despair and confusion from others, in all truth I found that the line between sanity and disorder to be a thin one that I wandered back and forth over far too often in my quest for resolution and understanding.

Certainly, there were times when it might have been easy to compromise, or even to end it all. Or, as a therapist once told me, sometimes there are just holes that exist in the mind, little psychological voids that can't be filled up no matter what but that if it ever became too difficult, there were medications one could take. Like lithium, for example, which smoothed things and made life bearable. But I didn't want things to be smoothed out and bearable. Not with hand-me-down answers, nor with drugs, or alcohol, or muddled mysticism, or Jesus, or ultimately, suicide. Even so, there were still far too many times when I didn't have any idea what it was that I needed but regardless, in that interim period after the divorce I did seek help. There were group therapy sessions at the local hospital in the evening. They were facilitated by what I assumed to be, two Grad students sharing the lead. The woman was clearly struggling with the responsibility, the man talked too loud and too much, as full of dictum as old Dr Freud himself and very soon, that was enough of that.

Next I went to another female psychologist but two sessions with her were all I could handle because I absolutely could not connect. No only did she seem to lack experience, she was also just not very bright. Disappointing as those encounters were, I left the idea of outside help alone and very soon after that met Sharon. It was new, intense, totally distracting and therapeutic in its own right, far more than enough to lift me up and turn me around. For a while, and for the most part, until I was well into the relationship with Sharon. Three years at least, perhaps a little longer. In a relationship but beginning to feel very lonely being there and it was then that I sought out another therapist. Not that it matters but her name was Lauren and she was special. Intelligent and intuitive, we covered a lot of ground together over the course of several months. Did it solve all my problems? Of course not. And while it certainly helped me to clarify my feelings and express some of my pain, it did not in any way help me resolve my situation with Sharon, someone I didn't want to leave but was finding it increasingly difficult to be with. Nor was that the entirety of it.

I had changed jobs for one thing and the new one was high stress and demanding. So was my father, but that was because of my mother. She was back in the hospital after a five year remission, had now been there for nearly two months. The hospital was just over a hundred miles away but I had still gone to see her several times.

And so, there I was again in mid February of that year, not knowing at the time that while she would still last another three long months even though it was the last time I would see her myself. Even then, however, when I went in I knew we were not alone in the room together. The grim reaper was standing at the foot of her bed, clearly not about to go away empty handed this time. That seemed more than obvious as I looked at her wasted body and listened to her labored breathing and wondered how I really felt about the situation. What would it be like to loose a parent? Would there be remorse, sadness, pain? Or after all this, only relief? She had been dying for several months now, giving ground a very small step at a time, all at the additional expense of those around her, particularly my father. Poor man, he was always in a state of panic. Understandably, they had been together for sixty years and on three or four other occasions I had gotten phone calls from him telling me that if I wanted to see her again I had best come right away because this was it. But still, I thought, as long as she was still alive, maybe it was a last chance for something. What exactly I was never sure. Like a lot of things, it wasn't clear anymore either. Maybe it was just because she was so afraid of dying. But why?

Where was her religion when she needed it the worst? Was there no blissful heaven, no Jesus waiting there with open arms to take her in and comfort her? Did she know that now, standing so close to the door, having gained a small peak at the real truth beyond? What would she do if heaven just happened to be full of a lot of other souls besides those of Christians? What if there were also Eskimos, Hindus, Muslims, a few Zulus and a stray agnostic or two wandering around, maybe even an atheist trying to keep things stirred up.

Religion had always been a point of dissension between us. I was the irreverent one, the heathen in the family, by her own definition. So what was I doing here at her bedside now if I was so bad, trying to console her? Where was the rest of the family? The good ones? Back in the midwest and up in Oregon, too far away. But, what the hell. Medicated as she was it was highly unlikely that she even knew who was and was not there and it was then that the doctor entered the room. Looking solemn faced, he said hello and put out his hand. I shook it and he began to talk. This is the way I remember the conversation.

"Have you made a decision yet?" he asked, referring to the fact that he had recently decided that maybe it was time to shut down the life support and let her go.

"It's not my decision to make," I told him.

"Well, she's your mother. Your father doesn't seem to be able to decide."

"Like I said. It's not mine to make."

"But, he said he was going to leave it up to you."

"Sorry. I can't do that."

"It would be the kind thing to do."

I shrugged.

"Can't you see she's in a lot of pain. It's not humane to let it go on when there's no hope."

"There wasn't any hope when you guys hooked her up to all that apparatus two weeks ago."

"We have a responsibility to the patient to extend their life as long as possible," was his answer.

"That's a bit contradictory don't you think?" I asked sarcastically. Now I was getting upset.

The doctor turned his back, lifted the oxygen tent, put his stethoscope on her chest, listened for a moment, pulled down the tent and stalked from the room. I watched him go, sure of one thing anyway. No matter what, I wasn't about to make my father's decisions for him no matter how angry he or the doctor became. Not when it involved another person's life.

But, yes, I had been through it all right, as my father had reminded me, acting as if that was supposed to have endowed me with some supreme wisdom or something. But it didn't and pulling the plug on my mother wasn't going to be my decision no matter what anyone said. And that is what I had told myself when a nurse entered the room.

"Well, how is she doing today?" she asked in an inane way as she picked up the patient chart whereupon I just turned around and left.

TOO MUCH

Too much job stress, too much caffeine, my body was in some kind of hyper state I couldn't seem to pull myself down from and by four o'clock on that particular day I felt like a hand grenade with the pin pulled, ready to blow. Then the phone rang for what seemed the fiftieth time. It was my father. Once again he was convinced that my mother wasn't going to make it through another night. And how many times had I heard that before? Four, five, six? And how many times had I responded appropriately and driven that more than the hundred miles down to the hospital? The same. And the crisis had always passed. But what about this time? Mother or not, I already come to terms with her passing so how many last times did I have to see her for the last time? But it wasn't about that, was it? It was about my father and what he needed. Or was it just what he thought he needed instead? I didn't know. But I could still clearly remember sitting alone in the hospital by my own wife's bedside at three in the morning when she slipped away. Would it have helped if someone had been there with me? Not to me. It would have been distracting and most likely would have detracted from the validity of the moment and distorted its significance. For me, it was better just to be alone with it for who else could truly understand how I felt anyway.

As for my father, however, I couldn't speak for him. All I knew at that moment was that, no matter what, I was just not capable of making the trip at that time. I was just too up tight, worn out, run down, frazzled and frustrated. And to have to drive clear across L.A. in rush hour traffic, it wasn't possible. It would take a least three hours just to get there. Maybe more. And then what? But I lied about it and told him I'd do my best. Too bad. I was going home early for a change, instead. Forget the damned problems. Then I remembered that Sharon and I were scheduled to go to a seminar that evening. One we had committed to some time ago. But it wasn't mandatory. I'd see how I felt. We could decide later.

Traffic was difficult, made worse by my cluttered mind. And if one more son-of-a-bitch in a BMW cut me off... Then I caught a glimpse of myself in the mirror. Haircut time again, long overdue. Might feel good too, to sit there and relax. Might as well stop, I decided. The intersection for the barber shop was coming up. I flipped on the turn signal and got in the left lane. Then the squeal of brakes, the sound of breaking glass and twisting metal and it was all over. Nobody hurt, just tore the front end off my car, that's all. No headlights, no grill, bumper totally bent out of shape, it was now barely drivable. Another problem to try and untangle. The cop came but couldn't verify the other driver's speed from the skid marks so I picked up the bigger fragments of my own car, threw them in the back seat. Not exactly in the mood to go home and try to explain what had happened just yet, I decided to get the haircut anyway. If nothing else, maybe it would help me relax so I pulled my battered car into the barber shop parking lot. Breathing hard, I went inside and sat down in the chair, got a trim, then a massage. Neither helped.

At dinner I began to notice a growing discomfort in my chest, a pressure and tightness. Not too unusual lately, however, I assured myself at the time. But Sharon noticed something was wrong, got up, came around behind my chair, began rubbing my shoulders and suggested that maybe we should stay home. I tried to relax but it seemed impossible and my discomfort continued to grow. I was also beginning to feel claustrophobic and seemed to be having some difficulty in breathing.. Needing to get out of the house, I said we should go to the event anyway. She disagreed but I insisted, not admitting how badly I really felt and not understanding what was happening.

By the time we reached Sepulveda Boulevard about four miles from home, the discomfort in my chest had become a dull pain. The dull pain rapidly turned into sharp pain and the sharp pain increased to excruciating pain. It reached from my chest to my back, across my shoulders, up into my neck and down my arms. Something beyond my control seemed to be squeezing the life out of me and there was nothing I could do about it except to tell Sharon to turn around and find a hospital.

Then I saw a liquor store sign and told her to pull in.

She didn't understand but stopped anyway. Somehow, over her objections, I got out of the car, went inside and bought a pint of brandy. Then I got back in the car, took a huge swallow and told her to get going. Frightened, she forced her way through traffic as I drained the entire bottle before we pulled up to emergency. As for the brandy, when it came to the pain, it might as well have been water. I was still stone cold sober. When it came to my heart, however, it might have been the stimulant that kept it pumping long enough for me to get past the night admissions clerk. I didn't have health insurance and there was absolutely no way she was going to admit me no matter what. She was not about to violate hospital policy. She could lose her job. An orderly came in and backed her up, saying that I could go to L.A. County hospital instead. That was down in Torrance. Only about twenty miles away. They could call an ambulance.

"To hell with it. I'll just die right here. Then what will you do?" I told her, getting angrier by the second. Something I really didn't need to be doing under the circumstances while poor Sharon just stood there growing more and more frightened by the whole ordeal and it was only then that I seemed to remember that a hospital couldn't refuse to admit a person with chest pains. Fifteen minutes of arguing until she finally called someone else to see if I was right. Fifteen critical minutes that might have cost me my life, may well indeed have cost me some additional damage to my heart. But then, finally, panic on the part of the staff as I was helped onto a gurney and rushed upstairs. And then I must have passed out because the only thing I seemed to remember was moving in and out of consciousness and more pain, time and time again, the only clear memory being that of me realizing there was window in the room and that if I could somehow have managed, I would have dragged myself over to it and jumped out. Other than that, nothing, which was also exactly what they were doing for me. Nothing. Only later would I learn the real truth.

The truth was that this hospital did not have a cardiac ward. There were no cardiologists on staff, either. Nor did they contact any. The only thing that finally saved my life was the fact that one of the resident interns just happened to recognize a visiting cardiologist from Cedars-Sinai in the hall after two days and had the good sense to seek his council, admitting they had no idea what to do with me. Frankly, I don't even remember the ambulance ride from there down to Cedars either, but somehow this new doctor was able to get me in the back door of that hospital and begin some proper treatment. Later he told me that he had no idea how I had survived those first few days at all and he was quite surprised to find me still alive even after the two days of the diligent treatment it took to finally get me stabilized in their intense care unit. An atypical situation. I wasn't in the hospital for just a few days or even a week either. Two days in the first hospital, twenty one more in Cedars-Sinai, still very weak and hurting, another small percent of heart tissue loss and I would have been dead for sure. Now it was heavy doses of prescription meds, fruit, fish and fowl as a diet, no driving, don't raise your arms above your head and get plenty of rest.

As for all that time in the hospital, who was it that came to see me after I was finally able to realize it when I had a visitor? My children for one. My ex wife for another and my old songwriter girlfriend. My business partner. A few other people I knew. But where had Sharon been all that time? I had no memory of her ever having been at the hospital at all. Was it that she was just too distressed and unable to cope? Like my father? I never even got a phone call from him and that hurt too, even though I could understand it better, what with my mother dying.

33

As for Sharon, however, there was also another twist to it. One that was rather bizarre. I could see why she might have been frightened and angry at me for almost dying on her but it was worse than that. While I was in the hospital she had gone through my desk and found a letter from an old girlfriend back east. Why I hadn't trashed it, I'll never know, but there it was for her to find. From someone I hadn't seen in years but who was coming to California that summer and if she could ditch her husband, could we get together? The truth was no, however. I hadn't cheated on Sharon, nor had I any desire to do so but she had assumed the worst and was also very angry about that.

Regardless, with me still in the dark about it, she was at the hospital on the day of my discharge and took me home with her where I climbed into bed to rest. And, so help me, no one could make this up but within half an hour the house phone rang. She answered and guess who was on the line? My sister, being thoughtful and concerned, had given this woman from the past our phone number and Sharon had immediately recognized her name. Then she threw the phone at me and hit me in the chest. Once I answered and knew who had called, I still had no idea of exactly what Sharon was so horribly angry about but I knew that if I stayed with her like this I'd be right back in the hospital. So, since my step son was the one who lived the closest, I asked him to come and get me.

ENDINGS

It took a week before Sharon finally called and we were back together again. But now what? Not only had she not come to the hospital, she had also put all my belongings into a storage unit. A place someone broke into shortly afterwards and stole most everything of value. But that wasn't the worst of it. Not only was I unemployed, I was now unemployable and would be so for months to come. I owed many thousands of dollars in medical bills. I did not have a back up savings account. My car was badly damaged and essentially undrivable. The state had revoked my drivers license saying I was without insurance. Not true but one more thing to resolve. But all in all, those were only details. The bigger problem was with myself. Not only was I physically damaged, I was psychologically destroyed and confused, needing things I had never needed before.

As for Sharon, my having a heart attack was absolutely not her fault. That is what she told me, anyway, right up front, which left me wondering why she would even consider it to have been in the first place. So what did her statement really mean now that I was weak and essentially valueless? Did it have something to do with our staying together? I had no idea how she felt about that either, now that I was largely disabled and it was then that I decided that somehow, impossible as it seemed at the time, somehow I was not going to stay around, become a burden and find out that way. But it was more than that. Other things had been building up between us too and, much as I disliked the idea, it seemed that long term I would eventually have to separate myself from Sharon and go my own way anyway. That became much more apparent when my mother finally died.

I was sleeping on my daughter's couch when it happened, trying to get by when I got the call. I wasn't surprised at the news nor that Sharon was the one who was telling me. Except for my children, everyone else still thought I was with Sharon. This included my sister who had called her house, thinking we were still together.

After telling me, Sharon asked how I was doing and would I be going to the funeral. I told her probably not unless I could find a way down. Hating to admit it, I still wasn't supposed to drive that far as yet. Doctor's orders, whereupon she volunteered..

At that point I remember trying to visualize her on the other end of the line, wondering just how sincere the offer really was. I couldn't tell. But still, she had known my mother too. Additionally, like it or not, I still missed Sharon regardless of everything else so I told her I'd accept before she could change her mind, thinking it would give us another chance to talk.

The chapel was over flowing with people and full of sympathetic smiles that would be good for my father, a man well known and well liked in his community. So too, all the perfunctory words the minister filled his eulogy up with. As for me personally, I had already resolved my mother's passing long before and didn't seem to be feeling very much of anything by being there, one way or the other. But still, after the service I got in line for that last walk past the casket. The right thing to do. I stopped briefly and looked at her. But what to say? Nothing, I guess. Too late for that too. Best to go find my father. See if we might come to terms with the situation between us. Then, with that partially resolved I got back in the car with Sharon and we headed home. Unfortunately, on the way I felt the need to sort through some of what had been going on between us, but it was a serious mistake because she refused to respond.

"No wonder we have problems," I finally said to her after a long silence, telling her how I thought we could never talk anything through. Even the petty stuff, wherein she informed me that we always talked about a lot of things.

I agreed but tried to make the point that the important ones were always the ones that were skipped over.

"Like what?" She had asked.

"Feelings, maybe."

"I know how I feel, she said defensively. "I don't have to discuss it with anybody. Don't you know how you feel?"

"Of course, dammit That's not the point."

"What is the point?"

"It would be nice to discuss some of the differences once in a while."

"Why? Aren't we entitled to have our own feelings about things?"

That was her comeback. Frustrated, I swore to myself. We were right back where we started. Why had she volunteered to come along? Obviously she was still angry about something. Couldn't she see what was going on between us or didn't she care? Now I was getting upset and I just blurted out that, "Love is a bitch."

"What?" she said, glancing at me.

"I said, love is a bitch."

"Why do you say that?"

"Look at us. I thought we had a lot going. The same view of the world, the same goals, we like the same things, some of the same kind of people, the sex always seemed to get better and better. Just one small problem."

"And what is that?"

"It's not what we talk about that causes the problems. It's the things we don't talk about," I tried to point out without success because, again, she didn't respond. More silence. Then, completely frustrated, I cursed out loud.

"You don't have to swear about it," she had said in return.

"Well maybe I want to swear about it for a change," I came back. "Maybe sometimes I just need to be able to say what's on my mind. Maybe sometimes I need you to listen to me like I was really here talking and have you hear me out and then respond to me like I said something.

Recognize me when I get on subjects you don't like instead of shutting me off and pushing me aside. If you don't agree with me, say so. Tell me why, so I can deal with it."

"So. What is it that you want to talk about?"

"For one thing, that stupid letter that you found."

She told me we had already talked about it.

"But it's still bothering you, so obviously we haven't talked enough."

"I'll get over it," she told me, the stubborn set of her chin letting me know it was probably going to be a long ride home, which it was. And that was to be contrasted with the fact that she called me two weeks later and invited me to go to a black tie event on Friday.

We went, kept it impersonal, had a good time and not only did I spend the night, but most of the weekend. Monday she would be going on a business trip, however, so on Sunday before I was getting ready to leave she told me a different story. During our last separation, she had gone to a resort in Mexico. Alone, she said, just to get away and think things through. But then, once there, she had gone down to the shoreline and began walking out into the ocean, not caring, and went too far. A life guard finally saw her and brought her back in, nearly drowned. So then, a bigger truth and an even greater dilemma. I had a woman in my life who had once told me back before the heart attack that if we got married she would put me on title and give me a half interest in her very nice house and loved me so much she didn't want to live without me but also someone who wasn't capable of helping me sort through my own greater issues and put my own life back together. Nobody's fault. That's just the way it was. So, how big of a compromise was I willing to make to be with her and where was I supposed to go from there?

DISOWNED

Sharon never said stay, she never said leave. It was my decision to make and it seemed she would accept it either way. But that didn't make it any easier. Regardless, side stepping that issue, all I can say is that the period directly following the heart attach was complicated and difficult. Simply put, by the end of the year the list of stress producing events was a rather long one. One that I can only summarize for now. In addition to the car accident and the medical problem, I had left my long term relationship with Sharon. I was in a financial crisis temporarily abated by multiple credit cards that only added to the problem. My mother died. I lived in eight different places that ranged from two stays back at Sharon's house to rental rooms, to my daughter's couch, to an old girlfriend's spare bedroom, to many weeks in a shoddy motel, to over a month in a warehouse. The year ended by me being the best man at my father's wedding when he re married and being told I was being disowned before that day was over, something which began with the best of intentions on my part.

After my mother's funeral I would drive down to see him periodically, spend a couple of hours together, play a few games of cribbage which he liked. Other than that we talked very little about anything important and nothing about what had transpired in either of our lives. My situation or his. Regardless, it was clearly obvious that after nearly sixty years of marriage he was feeling desperately lonely, depressed and in growing panic. Although he had other friends, was a member of the Masons and was involved with his church, none of it solved the problem of being alone in an empty house at night. Then, as reconstructed later, my father was targeted by a woman who belonged to the same church as he, possibly even before my mother was in the ground. I, however, knew nothing of this at the time. Nor did I know anything about it until about five months after my mother passed away when he announced that he was getting re married, and would I be best man at the wedding. It was two weeks away. Good for him, I thought. There was no prescribed amount of time for one to mourn the death of a mate and if that was what he needed to keep his life together, he should do it. But then, back at home I wondered, who was this woman. I had never met her or heard anything about her. As I soon found out, however, there was a potential problem. My father was debt free, owned the house he lived in and had a fair amount of money in bonds and in the bank while she was living with her married sister and all her combined assets consisted of a few clothes and a twenty year old car. Maybe that was okay and maybe it wasn't. Did he fully understand what he was doing?

Thinking it over, I went to see him a week before the wedding. By then the bride to be was there along with her sister and her sister's husband so after the introductions I asked him to come outside so we could talk in private. I tried to make it clear that I wasn't questioning his judgment   but did he understand about community property laws? Even though he was eighty years old, did he realize that he could still end up losing his house and a good share of his wealth if things didn't work out and maybe he should talk to his attorney before taking his vows. But no, he didn't want to accept that possibility. Instead he assured me they had already made arrangements to see the attorney after they were married to work out those details. Well, so much for that, I decided. But then as I looked around, there stood the bride to be's sister's husband, half hidden around the corner of the open garage door, close enough to have obviously having heard the entire conversation. Too late, I told him to go inside and leave us alone. Then I tried to re assure my father that I only had his own best interest at heart and left it at that. It was a mistake.

The big day came and I, dressed for the occasion, went directly to the church where the crowd was gathering. There, my father barely acknowledged me but as for everyone else, I was completely shunned. Even the minister had nothing to say. I was still best man, however. Too late for that to have changed, I guessed, so at the proper time I handed over the wedding ring and that was that. But then there was the reception at my father's house. Same situation, and by now it was more than apparent what had happened. The bride's brother-in-law had convinced the bride that I had tried to scuttle the marriage and she in turn had twisted it to where I was a complete villain, trying to ruin things for them both. The truth, however, was a bit different. When my father first told me he was getting married, he said that all he wanted was to live for another five years. That would be long enough, he said. But he couldn't do it living alone. So, for him, it was all about companionship. As for her, it was never clear but for sure in the end, it was a bargain made in hell where both were cheated.

My father got his five more years, however, plus another ten. He died at ninety six, what was left of him, but I was convinced that if he had been with anyone besides her, he would easily have lived to be over one hundred. She nagged him incessantly for one thing and complained to anyone who would listen that the marriage had never been properly consummated. Additionally, she became a complete burden medically. Some of it was obviously real, some not so much. At one point she claimed to be going blind and started walking around with a cane, feeling her way with the tip of it. On one of my visits my father and I were both in the living room talking while she was in the kitchen. Then she came and stood in the doorway and asked if anyone was in the room. Poor thing, she was in bad shape. Then, my father, whose back was toward her, answered, and she started out. I did not look in her direction either, but watched her peripherally as she headed in my father's direction across the large room. But then, directly in her path, there was the house cat, asleep on the carpet, about to be hit by her swinging cane. Except it didn't happen. The woman very deftly walked around the sleeping animal when she got to it, then went back to her cane, made it the chair my father was sitting in and felt around it to find him like she was completely blind. I have no idea how all that played out for them. Maybe she had been patted on the head by an angel or something in the meantime but by the time I next saw them over a year later, the cane was gone and she was finding her way around quite nicely. Regardless, real or not, her continuing problems compromised my father's desire to stay engaged with the rest of the world and wore him down even further. And then she tried to kill him.

They were now living in the retirement village run by the Masonic Lodge. A nice little apartment, two restaurants, a big campus, bus tours around the area and lots of other amenities my father was getting too infirm to even enjoy. Meantime, his wife's sister's husband, the weaselly little rat who created the earlier problem for me, had died and the sister wanted to move in with my father and his wife. Not possible according to the rules. But if my father was gone, maybe then it could happen, she reasoned.

It wasn't poison and she didn't try to push him down the stairs. It was much more subtle than that. I had gone down to see him near the end and spent the night, seriously wondering how he could still be alive from the way he looked. Very tired, he went to bed early and she left to go somewhere. About an hour later she was back and I was on the couch pretending to be asleep because I had absolutely nothing to say to her. She rummaged in the kitchen for a bit and then went into the bedroom which was adjacent to the living room where I was at and after few moments I heard her say, **heh!**, in a very loud voice. Then I heard my father rouse, mumble something and not get an answer. A few minutes later, after he was asleep again, the whole thing was repeated. And then it happened again and it was now very clear what she was trying to do. Keep interrupting his sleep and wearing him down till he passed away and who would know the difference. But now I did. I got up, went to the bathroom to let her know I was awake and could well have heard her. Back on the couch, I stayed awake for a long time to make sure it didn't happen again, wondering how long this had been going on. Obviously quite a while because he was much weaker and far more depleted than he was the last time I had seen him, not so long before.

The next morning, first thing, I went to see the manager of the facility, told her what I suspected and asked her to have the staff keep an eye on the situation, even though I knew there was literally not much they could do. Then I went back and talked to my father, privately, because she had gone to the restaurant for breakfast alone. Not only did I tell him what I thought was happening, I asked him for permission to speak to her about it. He agreed, reluctantly, I think. Regardless, I told her to sit down when she came back and started in. Angrily, I told her what I suspected, said that if it happened again I would be back with my attorney and she would be immediately out in the cold and furthermore there was no way her sister could come and stay with her, regardless, because it was against the rules. That done, I went to breakfast with my father, him weak and hardly able to walk. Then, when it was time for me to leave, he asked if everything was all right between the two of us. I said yes, and meant it. Two months later he was gone, and two weeks after that, so was she.

WANDERING

The following year started off in the same manor as the previous one had ended. An individual without a driver's license ran a red light and again smashed up the front of my now repaired car. That taken care of, a month later a big semi truck tried to change lanes on the freeway, didn't see me and ground a huge hole in the driver's side of my car with the big chrome lug nuts on his front wheel. And then, finally, a welcome surprise. Many years earlier my first wife and I had purchased a highly speculative piece of land in a small California town, and once paid for, literally forgot about it. But then, when my credit cards were all almost maxed out and two different collections agencies were sending me threatening letters, I got an offer on the property. As it turned out a new freeway now ran by it and it was located at what would soon be a major off ramp. It didn't make me a millionaire but it did put me in a position to negotiate. It also led me to find out that much of the medical profession is shockingly dishonest when it comes to money. Not so, the cardiologist who saved my life because he was as surprised as I was to learn that his partner, whose staff did all billing, was trying to charge me for two office visits which were listed as having happened before I had even met the man.

I could have pursued a lawsuit against the first

hospital also. But I didn't have the stamina for such a fight at the time so I let that one go when they reduced the bill by almost eighty percent. As for the very long stay in Cedars Sinai, that was a story in and of itself, and generally speaking for me at least, I thought it more like a house of horrors than a hospital and reinforced the maxim that if your going to be in the hospital, you need an advocate. As for what happened when I first went in and was totally drugged up, I can only guess. Later, in addition to all the disruption, noise and poor treatment, two things stand out as typical. Making her rounds one morning, the maid came into my room. First she checked the wastebasket. Then she went in the bathroom (which I could see into), cleaned the sink, cleaned the toilet and wiped up the floor, no rubber gloves on all this time. Then, lastly, without washing her hands, she took the pitcher which held my drinking water, re filled it and set it back down so I could reach it. Bad enough, but I was also still being medicated intravenously. As a result a steel catheter was left in one of the veins in my arm and taped down to make it easier to change fluids. But to reduce the chances of infection, the catheter was removed and replaced every few days.

On the particular day in question the nurse came into my room to do just that. First she pulled out the needle that is on the end of the small plastic hose that runs down from the fluid battle and laid it on the bed. Unfortunately, while she was getting ready to do that, the needle and hose end slipped off and fell to the floor. To keep it from happening again she picked it up and inserted the needle into the blanket that covered me. A bit unorthodox, I thought while reassuring myself that she would put a new needle on the hose too, when she was done. Then, back to the task at hand, she removed the old catheter, wiped down my arm with an alcohol swab, found a new vein

45

location, inserted the new catheter and taped it down. That done, she removed the needle from the blanket. But, instead of replacing the needle, she was going to re insert it into the catheter. I almost shouted.

She stopped, looked at what she had nearly done and, on the verge of tears, apologized profusely. Then she told me again how sorry she was but the hospital was under staffed and she had just worked three double shift nights in a row. Under the circumstances, the mistake was somewhat excusable on her part but what about the hospital? It was their responsibility to properly staff the place, especially in areas of critical care. But what if I had turned my head and hadn't watched what she was doing? What if I had been too tired or too medicated like I was earlier when I had first been admitted. The list of what ifs went on from there but it is no longer surprising to hear of people who go to the hospital to get well and end up being infected with something else even worse, or even dying.

At any rate, with that behind me and with money now in the bank, it was time to settle my account with this hospital too. But why was it so outrageously high? I demanded a fully itemized list of charges which ended up being over sixty full pages of IBM print out long. On and on it went, seemingly forever. But what was this? And this? And this? I got out a red pencil and went to work, underlining item after item. I must have had my arm shaved at least a hundred times with cheap plastic razors that they felt were worth many dollars each, two very expensive waffle pads I never got to sleep on, enough bandaids and bandages to patch up a platoon of soldiers in combat, enough intravenous fluids to fill a bathtub, x-rays and sonograms never received, blood work never done and more. It was outright fraud. Someone belonged in jail.

I went to the hospital accounting department, found the manager and made it clear that I was not about to pay their bill as issued. A week later I got the revised, essentially cut in half version in the mail. I paid it, leaving them to live with their lies, not mine to pursue any further. Then, debt free, I called a travel agent and spent ten days at a Club Med in Tahiti, along with some island hopping in small planes. An open ended trip, I moved on to Australia, then touched down for a few days here and there in such places as Bali, Bangkok, Singapore, Hong Kong and Tokyo. Generally speaking, I was far from being fully functional as yet and it was somewhat exhausting but I managed to survive and finally began to see some hope for my bedraggled condition.

Encouraged, I went on a Caribbean cruise which turned out well enough but then, back home, I began to philosophize. Although still medicated, lacking stamina and enduring some discomfort in my chest and an occasional pain or two, I was still alive. And I still had money in the bank that wouldn't be doing me much good if I dropped dead. That concluded, I called the travel agent again and headed back out over the Pacific. I would do it once more also but that particular trip gave me the best Christmas I had in years. I got on the plane in Los Angels in the afternoon of December twenty fourth, crossed the international date line around midnight and landed in Sydney on the twenty sixth, the lost day of no concern, happy to have avoided it.

A couple of months later I returned to Australia via Fiji where I spent several days, then roamed around the Australian outback on buses, went on to Hong Kong, opted for a two week tour of China and then came home, largely unmissed by anyone. No job, no relationship, no close friends anymore, children busily immersed in their own lives, so now what? Time to get back on the plane again. Only this time, head east instead of west, first stop London. Once again a, nothing planned, open ended journey. Rent a car in Ireland, take a boat up and down the Nile in Egypt. Ride a bus from Cairo to Tel Aviv, fly to Turkey, take an old cargo freighter ride across the Mediterranean from Greece to Italy, use my Euro rail pass to ride the trains in Europe. Trains, planes, buses, rental cars and ferry boats. In addition to Egypt, Israel and Turkey, I stayed in or went through every country in Western Europe, ended up in Helsinki and because there is no other way to do it, took a guided, two week tour of Russia. That done, it was back to Zurich and Vienna and then on to New York where, not wanting to go home to my nothing life, I flew to Florida and went snorkeling with a couple I had met in Florence. Delaying further, I then went to Wisconsin and rendezvoused with a woman from the past and finally, about four months later in all, there I was walking down Rodeo Drive again, wishing it wasn't over yet, never feeling so lonely in my life.

Unquestionably, it was a marvelous trip. For the most part I hadn't been a tourist, I had been a traveler. And certainly, while there were many times when it would have been nice to have shared it with someone special, it would have changed things dramatically. What I saw was mine alone, not elaborated on or distorted by tour guide interpretations or moderated by someone else's presence and opinions, well intentioned as they may have been.

The great Giza pyramid backlit by morning sun. Acropolis up on the hill, the mysteries of the past. Snow covered mountains rising up, majestic waterfalls tumbling down, black sandy beaches washed by the waves. Pacific atolls and turquoise water, the dark blue depth of the Baltic Sea. A little old man with long gray beard and sampan hat, a young girl walking in the rain, a graveyard with a million bodies buried under mounds of earth. Two little boys riding on a donkey, a small girl child begging for money. A tall black, regal Nubian woman standing by the side of the road, staring back at me. A lovely blond semi-goddess laughing at a friend. Sleeping on the floor in a strange airport, chasing after a bus, struggling with the many different languages.

Most everywhere a stranger, I rarely understood the language. Back home the chatter is forced on you in public places and gets in the way. All that mundane, petty stuff people go on about. But in a foreign country, uncomprehending, it is easy to tune it out and ignore, allowing your attention to spread outward to the larger scene. A blessing. At least until it's time to order something to eat. And then there was another twist to the language problem after a fourteen hour ride on a bus in Turkey to a small seaside town. There I was approached by a young man who had gotten a look at my blue passport back at the hotel I checked into and followed me down the street. Then, when I sat down at a table at an outdoor cafe, he came over and in almost unintelligible English asked if we could talk.

After some difficulty, I learned his story. Because of limited opportunity, he felt he needed to get out of Turkey. His immediate plan was to get a job on a tour boat and go on from there, but in order to do that he felt he needed to learn some basic English and could I help him with that? I must have shrugged at his request. I'm sure I did. From what he wanted and from where he was starting from, that seemed impossible under the circumstances. Besides, I didn't live there. I was just passing through on my way to somewhere else. And even though the where of that was yet unclear, it was never my intent to spend more than a day or two in some little Turkish town named Bodrum. That in mind, I offered to buy him lunch instead, thinking maybe that was all he really wanted anyway. That or some money.

But no, that wasn't it and he refused. English, he said

instead and nodded his head, a pleading look in his eyes. I patted my stomach. Nothing to eat last night and no breakfast, I was hungry so wouldn't he have some lunch too? No again, he insisted. But I did get him to accept a Coke and with that he took out a thick pad of paper and some pencils he had with him and started making notes in Turkish. That seemed like a hard way to get anywhere to me so I took the pad and a pencil and drew him pictures. Lots of pictures. A house, a car, a boat, a plane, a man, woman and child, on and on, each time printing the name in English alongside the sketch, giving it back to him so he could write the same word in his own language. Then I had him say it in English several times in a row. As many times as it took to at least make it marginally acceptable to my ear. It was tedious and challenging but then it turned into a fun little game for us both and before I realized it, we had spent nearly three hours together. A bright kid and an eager student, I agreed to meet again the following day.

The next day I asked him where he was living. He said in a tent out on the edge of town. Not a problem, the weather was good. Okay, I thought, and left it at that. And even though I would have liked to know more about his situation, we moved on to the more immediate task of learning English and spent another three hours adding to his notes. Not a problem, this still left me with more than ample time for me to explore this small resort town right on the Mediterranean and ordinarily I would have moved on at that point if I had some idea as to where to go next. But since I didn't, we met again on the following day.

It was then he told me someone had stolen most of his clothes the day before while he was away from his tent and that day he let me buy him lunch before we continued our work. After that, in the evening, I walked down to the harbor and there, anchored off shore, was a large cruise ship from Europe. And, out toward the end of the pier amongst the group of people gathered around, was my young friend staring out at the huge vessel. I left him alone, not wanting to interrupt his dream, hoping he now felt a little closer to achieving it and came back later to find another kind of boat tied up to the pier. I checked its destination and schedule. Tomorrow I would have to cut our session a little short because now I knew what I would do next. I would get on this large, Russian built hydrofoil that cruised the Greek Islands and see where it went. And while I traveled very lightly, I still went through my bag that night and on our last day together was able to give this eager student an extra pair of jeans, several T-shirts and pairs of socks which he was grateful for. But no money, absolutely he wouldn't accept that, even though it wasn't very much that I offered and was sure he could have used.

Another impressive young person was the woman I met on the old Greek freighter going across the Mediterranean from Greece to southern Italy. An all night trip, we sat up on the open deck and talked the entire time. From somewhere back in the American mid west, she had started out with her boyfriend. They were going to travel Europe for a month and then go home and get married. But after a week, he had had enough. Traveling was too stressful, it made him nervous and he wanted to go home. She, however, refused. It was what she wanted to do and she was going to take advantage of the opportunity no matter what, so they parted, nearly three weeks back by then. It was nice to see such certainty in one so young, wandering about, who I would meet again walking down the street in Copenhagen many weeks later yet, still by herself, still happy with what she had done and was doing. And then there was the language of music.

Pan pipes, flutes, rattles and drums, I first heard those

sounds one evening in Zurich. A troupe of musicians dressed in brightly colored native clothing from Ecuador, playing in the street, looking for donations to pay their way. And then, there they were again in the park in Athens, giving it their best. Coincidences do happen, of course, but what was this? Three times in a row because there they were once more in Copenhagen, no less, in the evening after I had re met the young American woman traveling alone. After that I explored Norway and Sweden briefly, then took another over night trip on a ferry boat across the Baltic Sea to Helsinki, Finland where not more than fifteen minutes later, it should have been no surprise, there was that music again.

As for the traveling itself, I can only say this. I had a good friend once. A woman with a most brilliant mind who lost the man she loved so desperately and went traveling too. Not hoping to find him, of course, because he had died. Nor to find his replacement. At first it just a major distraction which she had hoped would help make her memories fade away. But when they did not, it turned into a search instead. Something to bring back some meaning to her life. I could understand that need easily enough, because in my own way, I was searching too. And even though the "for what" part is not always clear, there are still days when I would love to lock up my house or give it away, get on a plane or a bus, or a train and keep on moving, wondering where that road would find its end. Never a worthless venture. Just a different kind of journey with its own set of rewards and possible peace. But in the end, for me at least, it's not about all the places one can visit. The towns and cities, man made wonders or natures far more grander scope but all in all, when all the traveling is done, that is not what I remember most. No, it was the special people I met along the way instead. Some of them fellow travelers, most of them not. Some of them give you directions and some give you a ride while others take you in, show you around and share a meal or two, nothing asked in return. Others, rarer still, became long term friends.

One of them was an Australian woman I met in Bali who later, along with the boyfriend I met later, asked me to stay with them and personally drove me all over south eastern Australia. Another person I met also gave me an excuse to do some additional, but more limited. traveling.

I flew to Toronto several times to see a woman I met on my Caribbean cruise and she flew to California where we explored most of the coastline by car and then went to Mexico together. After that, I slowed down and stopped to take another look at my life. What next, I wondered. At the rate I was spending it, my money might last another year. Maybe two at the most. Then what? Well, one thing was for sure. Above all, the last thing I wanted to do was to find a job and go back to work. Besides that, there really was one more place I still wanted to visit, this one most of all. If I could handle it physically, that was, since the altitude was around twelve thousand feet. That was in Cuzco and Machu Pichu. Was my heart now strong enough for that? After everything I had done since the heart attack, why wouldn't it be? Sure, I was very good at ignoring my aches and pains even if things didn't seem quite right once in a while but wouldn't I have dropped dead a long time back if something was seriously wrong? Probably, I tried to assure myself. But just in case..... I called and made the appointment. That led to the tests which caused my doctor to sum up my situation with those very few but very direct words. The ones where he told me that if he was me, he wouldn't go anywhere that wasn't across the street from a good hospital, which is where this story began.

NEW FRIENDS

I was fifty seven when I had the heart attack, I was fifty nine when I first got in my car and ended in up Sedona, Arizona. It was an entirely different place back then, before all the development and the tourists. Much smaller and more intimate on many levels. But the business owners and the real estate developers changed all that through the Chamber of Commerce which was determined to make the town a world wide tourist destination. And they did, which changed things dramatically. Of course the surrounding natural beauty was still there. Most of it. But it should have been made into a National Park and preserved in its natural state instead. Before all the developers did their land grabs and tore up a good share of the precious landscape with their bulldozers. They built a lot of high end houses too, but there is a tremendous gap between someone who wants a big house with a back drop of red rock cliffs to impress their friends with when they come to town and a person who was willing to live very minimally just to be there, experience the deeper mysteries of the canyons, not disturb the wildlife or destroy the habitat. For them, it was a spiritual journey instead, especially so back when I first started going there. Fortunately, however, it was not completely dominated by the nuttiness of New Age mumblings. The Harmonic Convergence was over. That two day, world wide meditational event had occurred two years earlier back in August of 1987 and was supposed to have raised the level of human consciousness to greater heights and transform humanity into something far more extraordinary than previously possible.

They called that spirituality also, which, to me, only makes me hesitant to use the word in general because of the many different connotations it carries, many bordering on complete disconnects from reality. There was a variety of those individuals who had landed in Sedona, too. Three different woman who all claimed to be the reincarnated Cleopatra, one Goddess Athena, an archangel Michael, Sakina- Keeper of the Wisdom, Sunshower (who once gave me her phone number but then told me I couldn't call her because she was living with another man) and some salesman who showed up and named himself Soaring Eagle. Soaring Eagle claimed to be the most powerful because he could make is stop snowing when it suited his purpose and he had come to Sedona along with a guy called Wisdom Bear. Their mission was to reconnect the three major vibrational power spots in the area which would finish the job begun by the Harmonic Convergence meditators and transform the world even further.

Energy vortexes had already been invented by then also. They were composed of subtle energies emanating from the earth and were supposed to affect anyone who came within a quarter mile, resonate with their inner being and improve their psychic wisdom. This lunacy even progressed to the point where one can now get a guided tour to these fictitious anomalies. Of course some people will still swear by them. One couple even avoided paying their bill at a very expensive resort located adjacent to a "vortex" because the wife complained that the energy was so strong she wasn't able to sleep the whole time they were there. It seems no one bothered to ask them why they didn't go elsewhere after the first night or two. Regardless, people continue to make claims about such things and some seem gifted with their ability to sense them. Or cursed. Not only are there healing energies and consciousness raising energies, there are also noxious energies and woe to the unlucky individuals who are susceptible to them. Not only will they interfere with your sleep, they will also make you ill and cause bad things to happen in your life in an ongoing way. But while you can't turn off an energy vortex if it affects you adversely, you can do something about noxious energies. Just ask the experts.

They will gladly sell you little blue beads of glass which you can attach to your phone, your microwave and other appliances. Then, since they are so talented, they will come out and dowse your property, not to find water or minerals but to see if you are unfortunate enough to have a noxious energy stream running under your house, perhaps even right under your bedroom which is especially serious. If this should be the case, don't worry. For a few extra dollars they can use some metal rods and a hammer and move this underground hazard to a new location. Then, to further improve the situation one should then sprinkle a circle of crushed blue colored glass completely around the outside of the house and complete the job with strips of blue masking tape put down across all exterior doorways. And just in case, maybe a strip across the sills of any windows one might want to open.

While some see life as conspiratorial and out to get them in this directly personal sense, there were other equally overt and deeply rooted, but much wider reaching conspiracies afoot at the time also, not only in the Sedona area but country wide in proportion. They had to do with the U.S. government. First there were the black helicopters. Secondly, more than one person claimed to know someone who had seen Russian troops on the trains that came through Flagstaff and the theory was the government was spying on everyone and was going to make a large portion of the Verde Valley, where Sedona is located, into a major concentration camp with the help of the Russian soldiers who would be guarding us. This was important because it is more effective to have inmates guarded by foreigners than with their own people. Not me, maybe, because since I was new in town, a little older and somewhat reserved, I also had a couple of people ask me if I was with the CIA or some other sinister government agency. Unfortunately, in spite of all the claims, no one actually had any photographic proof of these foreign troops loose in our midst. As for the black helicopters, however, yes, they did exist and there was a period where they came to Sedona on a regular basis. But they were not there to spy on anyone or help incarcerate them. There mission had a different purpose.

They landed at the Sedona airport to refuel and give the special forces guys a chance to have breakfast. Then they would fly off into the surrounding mountains to practice tactics, not to conquer the local inhabitants but because the terrain was similar to that of other locations around the world where there were armed conflicts that the U S was, or soon would be, engaged in. Iraq for one and later Kosovo for another. Then there was and still is that group of people who are taking a more direct approach in dealing with their paranoia. These are the home grown militia and almost every state did have and still has one or more organized assemblage that spends a lot of money on guns and ammunition, along with time in the woods shooting rubber bullets at each other. That the local ones are still active is evident almost every morning when I step outside because I can hear them popping off round after round in the distance. As for my own opinion of this matter, I think that while most of them may be a little skewed in their outlook, they are still relatively sane in the way they choose to express and defend their own independence. They also make the statement that if worse ever came to worse, not everyone would just lie down and allow themselves to be trampled over. Independent thinkers are an important part of a healthy society too.

Well, beyond that and fortunately for me, this was but a small part of the Sedona I came to know. On the more basic side of things my first Sedona friend, Mary Kay, also introduced me to the books of a most controversial author. His name was Edward Abbey, naturalist, environmentalist, Forest Ranger, bulldozer hating anti-development agitator, the man who would have personally obliterated Glen Canyon Dam, could he have done so. The man made structure whose presence covered up and destroyed some of the most beautiful scenery in the entire world. Not only did his books broaden my perspective immensely, they made hiking and my own modest excursions into the wilderness a new adventure entirely. Beyond being something of irreplaceable grandeur, mankind's long term survival depended on its preservation. So inspired, I sat down a year later and wrote my own version of a sequel to Abbey's books. But my main characters didn't resort to sabotaging bulldozers and blowing things up with dynamite, they went hi-tech instead. They invented an invisible, high power laser that could burn through concrete and steel and not only shut down the Three Mile Island generating plant but completely destroyed the interior of Hoover Dam.

Prior to this and before I actually moved there, but after Mary Kay moved to Flagstaff to go to college, I returned to Sedona periodically to stay for a week or two to hike and explore. I also checked out the night life in the cowboy bars. What I liked about them was that, while most everyone was friendly, no one ever asked where you were from, what you did for a living, what kind of car you drove or any other status related questions. They either liked you or they didn't and it went on from there. These places were crowded on weekends when they had live entertainment but a bit slow otherwise. But that wasn't necessarily bad. Like the quiet night I walked into a nearly deserted place out on the edge of town and sat at the bar. Down a ways sat an old Indian with a weather beaten face and beside him a much younger woman I thought might be his daughter. Long, dark, straight hair, big brown eyes, probably as tall as he was but slim and trim. They talked very little and didn't stay very long and shortly after they left I got up too and went back to my motel up on the mesa at the airport.

The next morning I went down to the local coffee shop for breakfast and who should my waitress turn out to be but the woman I saw in the bar the night before. I said hi and things moved on from there. The old man she had been with at the bar wasn't her father, they shared a house together, along with a sometimes boyfriend she soon evicted. She wasn't native American either although the old man had influenced her thinking somewhat. He had come to the Sedona area from Minnesota with a specific purpose in mind. Tribal leaders from around the country came together periodically to discuss the social and political situation of the times and decide on courses of action. According to old legends the Red man knew in advance that the White man would come and take their lands, decimate their culture and destroy their people. Eventually, however, the day would come when the White man would be in serious trouble socially and environmentally and would need help. At that point key individuals from the Native American world would leave their tribes and move out into the White man's domain to share their wisdom and attempt to influence enough people to make a difference.

A very noble mission I thought, when I first heard of it, but wasn't it also a little naive and rather grandiose? How could a few individuals like this old man ever make a significant difference in a world so oblivious? It didn't seem possible even though it did have an impact of sorts on some people of that generation. Part of it came from some basic misconceptions as to what being an Indian was really all about and, if one should be so lucky as to have some native blood running in their veins, what that would automatically have endowed them with. Wisdom and a level of spirituality a white man was not capable of achieving on his own. As a result many young, and some not so young, men and women both, became wanna-be Indians, thinking that if they pounded on their drums and danced around the fire long enough, smoked unfiltered cigarettes and learned to say Mitakuye Oyasin properly, they could sneak in the back door and get there anyway. Mitakuye Oyasin is a widely used, borrowed phrase from the Lakota tribe which reflects their belief in the oneness of all forms of life. All things are related and we should live in harmony with them. Unfortunately, too many of the people I met during that period had no idea as to what what the words really meant. To them it was like saying amen at the end of a prayer, hoping that if that add on was made, the prayer was more likely to be honored. Also unfortunate were the limitations exhibited by the old Indian elder who had come to Sedona to help save the world, the one who was sharing an apartment with the woman I would end up with in another very special relationship. Before going there, however, let me divert.

To say that all things are related, both the living and the non living is one thing. To take it a step further and say that all living things, from the tiniest insect to the largest animal and from the smallest blade of grass to the tallest of trees, deserve respect is even more. But to scoff at the idea that everything is alive, even the rocks, may be a mistake because, as science progresses, the line between what is considered to be living and what is not becomes more and more blurred and impossible to clearly define. Some very eminent scientists have even made the statement that "matter is not inert. It is alive and active."

This is a viewpoint science is sharply divided over,

however, with those on the other side of the issue still proclaiming that the universe was and is a purely accidental happening. This means that even though matter sometimes behaves in bizarre ways, it is still totally inert and lifeless and that because everything is the result of a great cosmic accident, life does not have a built in, inherent meaning to it, that dead is dead and in the interim humans have to invent the codes of conduct they choose to live by. This is where their logic leads them. I, for one among the growing many, strongly disagree because their conclusions are only logical if a preponderous amount of other evidence is ignored along the way. Regardless, provable or not and however ancient it may be, I began seeing the Red man's view of life as conceptually beautiful and important, just like that of the Australian Aborigine and the black man living uncorrupted in the wilds of Africa along with the native living out of civilizations sight in the jungles of South America and in other places around the world. A philosophy that promoted respect for all life forms, no matter how we may decide to define them, and just as importantly, for the planet itself, the one we live on. Not that I didn't always feel that way to some extent myself. But, melting glaciers, rising sea levels and drastically altered weather patterns made me even more aware of the effects of severe over population and the future of the human race, everyone included.

Nevertheless, getting back to my story of that time, I found the following to also be true. While being a member of a particular race might endow a person with some of it's traits, it did not automatically endow them with the same level of insight and the depth of wisdom exhibited by some of their forefathers. Regardless, as stated previously, many young white men and women still seemed to think so and became wanna-be Indians in the process, borrowing words and rituals alike in their quest and catering to almost anyone who came along who fit the role. Some misguided women even went to bed with them, thinking that that kind of infusion might be a shortcut way of gaining a more heightened spirituality. Fortunately for me, my new found friend, even though she shared a house with the old indian, did not see things that way and had her own unique view of the world.

Her name was Dee and she talked to the ravens. One of her raven friends, an especially big old male she called Heath, used to sit on the lamppost outside the grocery store and squawk at her when she came by and would fly down to pick up the peanuts she would toss on the ground. Another thing she liked to do was to hike and explore and I found it to be especially charming when we were alone in some remote area for her to go both barefoot and topless. As for the ravens, we had another very unusual encounter with them also. Perhaps by chance, perhaps not. But later after I finally moved there.

We had been riding around the back roads and stopped to climb a bald, dome shaped hill for no other reason than it was there. Up top, having stopped to rest and check out the view, we heard the flap of wings and watched a pair of ravens land not too far away. Then more came. Alone, in pairs and groups of three and four, they kept coming and coming, surrounding us in a sea of strutting, squawking and chattering black, moving in close, some not more than a few feet away. Easily, there had to have been at least a hundred of them and probably more. But why? What did it mean? Wild birds checking out a pair of humans? Was it because of her? Maybe it was her old friend Heath from the lamppost back in town showing us off to his feathered friends. A most unusual experience, nonetheless, and I felt honored to have been a part of it.

We had other adventures also. As said earlier, I first

saw this women in a bar with an old Indian and again the following morning in the coffee shop where she worked. I asked to see her that evening and did, and the next day returned to California for a doctor's appointment. He said I wasn't out of the woods yet but to keep doing whatever it was I was doing because it seemed to be working. True enough, I was feeling better than I had in a long time, made even more so by what happened when I returned to Sedona. My new friend Dee took an open ended amount of time off from her job, we got in my car and drove north on what was to be our get-acquainted trip. We visited Monument Valley and then continued on up into the voodoo land of Utah's spectacular rock formations and awesome scenery. We took short hikes in five different National Parks, rented a power boat and explored Lake Powell where a thunderstorm almost washed our tent away in the middle of the night, spent another night sleeping in the woods on the north rim of Grand Canyon, feed the mule deer out of our hands in Zion, watched the cowboys rounding up cattle in the high country and stopped in a dozen different places along the back roads on the way home. Then I found a rental house in the old town part of Sedona and she went to California with me to pick up a fifteen year old Ford van I had acquired in a bad business deal which technically cost me seventy two thousand dollars, loaded it up with my possessions and came back to Arizona.

Our next adventure was on New Years day. It was quite warm out so we decided to go for a short hike and she picked the location. We began at the foot of Horse Mesa and soon came to a sign that said, Hot Loop Trail. Good. A loop is a loop so if we took the trail we should somehow end up right back where we started. By now it was about one o'clock but, no problem, we thought it was doable. Two hours later we began to question the loop sign. First we ran out of all marks of any real trail. No footprints, no worn pathway, just rocks, but we kept on. Another hour, however, and the situation was becoming undeniably clear. Up until then the route had kept curving around to our left, but now it started curving right so if this was indeed a mesa, it was a very long one. Unfortunately it would also be getting dark in another hour which left us with little choice but to turn around and re trace our steps. Or, guessing at how far we had walked and where we might be geographically, the quickest way out might be to go up and over the top. But up was several hundred feet of very steep, rocky incline and did we really want to do that?

We did. And that took a lot longer than we expected because it was so rough. How long, we couldn't be sure. Neither of us wore a watch. We didn't have any water with us either, or something to snack on and only light clothing because the day had been so warm. Pretty stupid for sure and then, by the time we made it all the way up, it was getting dark. No time to waste, we picked a direction and started walking, no leisurely pace this time. But it was not as easy as down below. The top of the mesa had snow on it. The snow had melted enough during the day, however, to make the ground we walked on muddy. No boots either, just sneakers and soon our feet were wet and cold as darkness overtook. Cigarette lighter, matches, something to start a fire with? Never thought of that either. But then, lucky us. No sooner had it gotten dark than there was the moon, nearly full, coming up behind us, filtering through the trees, telling me that at least we were headed in the right direction. Even so, she started to get depressed and worried as we stumbled along, wondering how long it would take before someone found our bodies because even if someone missed us we hadn't told anyone where we were going to begin with. So, to break the mood, I asked her questions, got her to sing some songs and keep on going, me in the lead and then, what was this?

There were footprints in the snow and mud. At least we were on a trail and that, I assured her, had to take us somewhere, and that seemed to help. Finally, a long time later, tired, starting to shiver a little, the moon now fairly high in the sky, the top of the mesa sloped downward and, off in the distance, I could see the notch in the next row of lower hills that we had come through many hours early when we began our hike, but still at least another mile away. That meant going down another step slope to get off the mesa we were on, climbing over another small hill and going through two barbed wired fences in the dim light before we arrived at our car. But we did it and our brief afternoon hike become a nine hour adventure to be laughed at later. Lesson learned, however. The next time we hiked I brought alone my new canteen filled with water and a back pack stocked with matches, hunting knife, compass, flashlight, extra batteries, rain gear, leather gloves and several other sensible items. Later I added a hundred feet of rope after finding myself up on top of steep slopes I almost killed myself on trying to get back down. As for my friend Dee and I, while we had many more unique adventures, one in particular was potentially just as serious. It was after some heavy rains and the streams and rivers were running full.

We took the canoe I had built several years before, went down to the Verde River and put it in the water. She said she had canoed before and knew how to paddle so, with her in the front and me in the back, the intent was to move upstream as far as we could go and then drift back down. Surprisingly, we actually made it about a quarter of a mile before her strength gave out. At that point the front of the canoe came back around and we were carried sideways down the river, her end closest to the shoreline.

Bad enough but just downstream a very tall old tree had fallen over and its branches reached well out into the water, right in our path. The front of the canoe hit first, the canoe flipped over on its side and tossed her up into the branches of the tree while I was dumped into the cold water and swept under the tree where my wristwatch was torn off and my sweatshirt got caught in the branches. Somehow I struggled free, however, leaving my sweatshirt behind and emerged on the down stream side, cold and out of breath, finding my friend quite distressed because she thought I had drowned. Not me, however. I just laughed very loudly. Not so much because I hadn't drowned but because I hadn't had another heart attack from the excitement and cold water shock. But I didn't tell her that. Other than those back in California who already knew, I didn't tell anyone I had ever had a problem with my health and I wasn't going to. Call it pride, call it something else. Privately I'd take my prescriptions and follow the rules for getting well but I'd drop dead before I'd play off of my weakness. But then, about a year later, I reconsidered.

I didn't like the side effects of the meds I was told I would be on for the rest of my life. They sometimes made me feel fuzzy headed like I was an early Alzheimer victim and that was very annoying. So was a restricted diet, along with the idea that I shouldn't be doing anything extreme, which I had been trying hard not to do. So, what happened? One morning after I woke up, I had a weak cup of coffee, took out a bowl and reached for the cereal box. But, god, I was tired of cereal. And yogurt and a whole lot of other things so I got up and threw it in the trash. Then I cleaned out the refrigerator. That done I opened the cupboard and looked at all the damn pill bottles. Prescription medicine, some CoQ10, vitamins, minerals, herbal supplements, every last bit of it. It all went in the trash too. Then I went to the coffee shop, ordered some bacon and eggs and never looked back.

A couple of years later, after eating what I wanted, when I wanted, taking longer, more demanding hikes and other activity, I stopped to see my old doctor on a trip back to California. He was a bit shocked, I think, after I told him how I had disobeyed all his instructions and he looked at the EKG he had just run. I had a very healthy heart and there was no indication whatsoever that anything serious had ever happened. How that could have been possible, he didn't know. As for myself, personally, I developed my own theory. Looking back, I believe that what really saved my life was getting in my car back when I got the really bad news and driving off in desperation without a goal in sight because it led me to a new location and an entirely different way of life. No big city congestion, noise, aggravation, smog and night time city glow that hide the stars from view. And, except for Phoenix, in Arizona the sky was blue and it had big white fluffy clouds in it. And there were red rocks and huge cacti and tall trees and sunsets. God, I loved the sunsets. But even more than, it was the new people I was lucky enough to have met when being there. These were the things that helped to keep me from fully accepting my own condition or integrating any such ideas into becoming a part of my personal identity. Suddenly awed and inspired by my new environment, I refused to see myself as damaged or limited and shut out any such ideas when they came up, challenging myself to walk a little further, stay up a little later and seek out new experiences. My friend Dee was more than helpful in that regard.

For one thing, Dee and the old indian Hollis, held Talking Circles in their living room every week which always attracted a group of people. Holding the Talking Stick, Hollis would usually lead off on some topic, people would raise their hand if they wanted to respond and the stick would be passed to them. Of course the stick didn't talk. Not even an old American Indian elder can make it do that. It was used to maintain order instead, where only the person in possession could speak and it worked quite well. There was no time limit on the meetings, either. They lasted until people got tired and started to go home.

Generally, the discussions were about common sense things, sprinkled with a little indian lore. What would you do if this happened and, what about that? Nothing ever very profound and in my opinion, it would take a lot more than this to get the rest of western society to change their ways. Still, Hollis, probably in his seventies at the time, was cordial enough. Young people liked and confided in him, making him more of a misbegotten guru than anything else. One such person was a much younger married woman who started coming to the meetings and ended up leaving her husband, buying a house from the divorce settlement money and letting the old man move in with her. Like the psychologist sleeping with the patient, that seemed a bit contradictory to me but.... Old indians were in demand back then, however, and people sought them out to come and speak or just to have around to bolster their own image. A special center piece for the dinning room perhaps. At any rate, his true form emerged when he was lured back east by another group of people, leaving the little maiden behind to try and put her life back together. As a Native American and as an individual, he was to be contrasted with someone else I met at the time. That person's name was Two Birds.

Two Birds came to town after Hollis had been there a couple of years, not to save the white man or the world, but because that was where he ended up, having found out that he could make a little money giving speeches and conducting week end retreats. Younger than Hollis, with a deep voice and a far more powerful presence, he commanded attention and spoke well as we learned from going to a presentation of his. A unique individual to be sure, he was a Vietnam war veteran who had been overrun and left for dead on two occasions. He had also had Agent Orange dumped on him. That's what sucked the strength out of his bones and eventually put him in the grave. Somehow, however, after his discharge, he had gone to college, got a masters degree in psychology, taught at the University of Nebraska and wrote a volume of poetry. He also took part in the American Indian Movement and was arrested for trying to smuggle guns into Wounded Knee where the Indians were engaged in a standoff with the FBI. The rest of his background is sketchy and never seemed important. What is, however, is what he brought with him when he came to Sedona, something which old Hollis lacked entirely. That was ceremony.

Two Birds was a pipe carrier. This meant that he had been given a, considered to be sacred, redstone ceremonial pipe that he could use in the Native American traditional way to perform ritual and ceremony. The origin of the redstone pipe had its own legend attached to it. As the story goes, it was given to the Lakota several hundred years ago by a white woman who was either a spirit form or a visitor from outer space, had a great deal of symbolism built into it and was to be used in a peaceful, healing way. Many other tribes also use the pipe for similar purposes in their own versions of ritual but to be of any value and have any power, or medicine, the pipe must first be awakened in a special ceremony dedicated solely to that purpose. Where Two Birds got his "medicine" pipe, I have no idea but he respected it and had faith in its power. And when he used it he did it in a solemn and most impressive way, whether it was in the backyard of his rental house in west Sedona, out in the woods somewhere or up on the side of the mountain where he later lived.

As for Sedona itself, it was a much different town back then. Smaller and with a different focus. A place where people came in search of something other than a big house in a gated community. Something not always clearly seen as several people shared a cheap rental property instead, or lived out in the national forest in a tent, or in their car, maybe even in a cave, some of them by choice, others out of pure necessity. I came to understand what that experience was like because I also went through it myself on two different occasions. In my case I termed it semi-necessity. The first time was after being there for a year. I wasn't flat broke but I would be if I kept renting houses to live in. I could have had a room in someone else's home but that just didn't appeal to me so I put my belongings in storage and lived in my truck for six months. Then I found another less expensive rental house, stayed there for six months and then went back to my truck for over a year.

On the up side, that had a certain freedom to it. As long as I had money for gas and food, I was free to roam wherever I wanted. And I did by exploring a multitude of back roads throughout the southwest. Among the many things I learned from that experience, one of the more important ones was that I could survive without television and for several years I never had one or knew anyone who did. And what affect did that have on my life? None that I could see. Presidents, politicians and world leaders came and went while all the rest went round and round. The names changed but the stories were essentially all the same. But not having to work was the biggest bonus of all. No one to be accountable to, bosses, stockholders or customers, not even the IRS. And while the president may be considered to be the most powerful man in the world and someone else the most powerful man in Los Angeles or New York or even in Sedona, as long as I didn't break any serious laws, none of them had any power over me.

It could be argued, however, that more money would bring an even bigger freedom because one could be flying around the world instead of riding around in an old truck. But in my case, it didn't seem to matter. I had already mingled with movie stars and rubbed elbows with tycoons and knew that their lives could, and often did, become just as much of a trap as anyone else's. Besides that, where does it say that a person has to be gainfully employed, pay taxes and be a contributing member of society instead of sleeping in the woods or hanging out on the beach all day. And while some may think those kinds of people are harming themselves by living the way they do, they are at least not harming others as they learn the life lessons that are important to them. Many of the super rich don't pay taxes either and have lived their lives as predators, stealing from others. Legally or illegally, it makes no difference. Other than consolidating wealth, of what value is their contribution to the world unless guilt catches up and they create charities and foundations to return some of it back into the system they preyed on. Of course most of it is still a matter of viewpoint. But at that time, and in the situation I was in, I was certainly changing a lot of my personal opinions about almost everything and ultimately, regardless of their financial situation or social status, I came to respect many of the wayward people I had met as much or even more so than a lot of those leading what would be considered to be, more normal lives.

On the downside of roaming around, however, there were times when it was also nothing more than miles and miles of loneliness, often eating something out of a can that was warmed up on the propane stove after having found a safe, out of sight place to sleep at night. But still, generally speaking, there was always a new town to stop in and new people to meet. Or perhaps an old town revisited. Take Tombstone, Arizona for example. The first time I walked down Main Street there, it was complete dejavu. I swore I had been there before in some past life time even though I never met anyone there I might have known back then. Still, I met several local people I liked and returned several times. And while I often still felt lonely and rootless at times it didn't drive me into depression even though the immediate impact was sometimes severe. Like the year I visited my sister in Colorado at Christmas.

Coming back to Sedona I got caught in a snowstorm, barely made it through before they closed the highway and arrived in the middle of the night. But there was no one to call, or to take me in or to even let know I had returned. No private bathroom or shower to step into either, no one to snuggle up to, no electric blanket on the bed. Just two sleeping bags in the back of the truck, one stuffed inside the other to keep warm, waiting for morning to go down to the coffee shop to see if anyone was around that I might say hello to, friend or not. My problem, somehow I'd get through it. My children and other family members didn't need to know about it. Even so, if it was painful for me it was nothing as bad as that of a middle aged, homeless woman I met who had everything she owned in the back seat and trunk of her car and had to sleep sitting up because the vehicle was too small and overloaded to stretch out in. That was when I really felt sad. But she, even so, still seemed undaunted. Better than being trapped in downtown L.A. sleeping in a cardboard box any day, she said. Breathing clean air and listening to the coyotes yipping and yapping in the night was far more reassuring to her than the stink of automobiles and the sound of sirens echoing through the streets by far. And then she was gone, I never knew to where, but inspiring nonetheless.

Later I would be lucky enough to meet another such woman who was even more brave, along with many other kinds of convention defying people who came to the area at that point in time. Family and jobs left behind, they came as though willed to do so from out of the past, to renew some enigmatic, previous life connections, think about the great mysteries, re examine the spiritual side of self, stay awhile, then slowly disappear, one by one, back into more normal society, hopefully better because of what they had participated in when they were here. Some of that was ritual. In addition to going on long hikes out in the canyons, they gathered at medicine wheels, built bonfires, lit sage bundles and smudged each other, had drumming sessions on moonlit nights, put together sweat lodges and looked for meaning. Much of that was possible because of the efforts of one particular individual, a middle aged white man no less, with his own expanded view of things. His name was John.

John's story of how he happened to end up in Sedona was also unique, just like my own and that of many others who showed up. He lived back east and one day a woman he knew came by, said she was going west to Arizona and would he like to ride along? As a result he put all his stuff in a storage unit and off they drove, ending up in Sedona where he stayed, never bothering to ever go back and claim his property.

Career wise, John was a geologist who lived in his battered, twenty year old van when he was in town, usually had a beard that would have put Rip Van Winkle to shame, wrote computer software used in deep earth oil explorations and sometimes taught summer classes at the University of Miami. He also hiked several hundred miles of the John Muir trail, climbed Mt. Whitney, ran for city council and published a bi-weekly, free newsletter that was available around town. Most importantly, however, was the fact that he was instrumental in creating a very large medicine wheel on the huge flat rocks half way up the hill on the east side of town. This was before the city merchants convinced the forest service to start requiring citizens to have a permit to park on public land, the obvious intent of which was to discourage people from sleeping in their vehicles and get them out of town. These strange non conformists might scare the money spending tourists away and that just couldn't be.

Regardless, the medicine wheel had a large fire pit in the center and when the moon was full, John and his friends would go up the hill, start a bonfire and begin to drum. Then, somehow getting the word, other people would show up too, and it became an ongoing ritual. John's lady friend would light a sage bundle and smudge them with smoke before they could take a place around the circle and allowed to drum. Often times there would be thirty or forty people up there, and a few times fifty or more, some from as far away as New Zealand or Germany. How they learned of it, we could only guess but when the fire was raging, sparks flying up into the air, the moon coming up over the mountain and the sound of dozens of drums all pounding out a beat in unison, it was a mind altering, awesome experience to be sure. And for some of us, one that lasted well past the middle of the night as we continued on, then slept on the rocks for a couple of hours before going home, whatever that meant for some.

Beyond that, John also started something called "encampment" where a group of people would go camp out in the woods for several days in a row. There they talked, built fires, danced, sang songs, drummed, cooked communally and slept in tents, cars or on the ground. The first one only had about a dozen people in it and only lasted three days. The final one a few years later had over a hundred people in it and lasted a week, some individuals attending from as far away as Vermont, having somehow heard about it. And as if that wasn't enough, the other thing John did was to finally rent a house with his lady friend where they lived for six months before they separated. While there, he built a sweat lodge in the back yard and conducted ceremonies on a regular basis that many people participated in. Not me, though. I would tend the fire and carry hot stones but I wouldn't go in the lodge at the time because I wasn't sure all that heat, steam and closed in air would be good for me.

As for John, however, he did what he did, modestly and generously, never seeking credit for any of it. He didn't council people either, never played the role of guru, priest, rabbi, shaman or life coach and expressed himself through his actions rather than through words. Regardless of that when looking back, in my opinion he was probably one of the more influential people of the time for those who came in quest of something other than the ordinary. Like myself, for example. My Sedona experiences with such unique individuals, along with hiking and living in my truck, not only brought me closer to the natural world but also helped me redefine my own list of personal priorities along the way. Career success and money were no longer important. I needed the opportunity to meet more unconventional people and the time to explore new ideas, philosophize and reconsider most everything that had gone before. That also meant engaging in new experiences. One of these was to have a vision quest.

Traditionally another American Indian rite, I still wanted to do one of my own. If possible, it might best have been done under the supervision of a Native American in an epical manner. But old Hollis didn't participate in such things and Two Birds was not around at the time, so I decided to improvise. That done, I drove out to a remote area, climbed up on top of the red rocks where no one was sure to come, spread out a sleeping bag to sit on and took off all my clothes. It was the middle of July, searing hot in the day but comfortable at night and I was able to stay there for two days and two nights. It was supposed to have been four but I made one serious mistake.

As prescribed, there was no food. But, I had brought along a large supply of water, thinking it necessary because of the heat. Regrettably, that was the mistake, because the more I drank, the hungrier I got, to the point where it became absolutely unbearable and I gave up. Anyway, just as well because a few years later Two Birds moved into an isolated log house up on the side of a mountain in New Mexico and started a small community of his own where vision quests were encouraged. But then, as I found out, when formally done, it was a complex process. There were five of us who were going to make the attempt and first we each had to find a site which suited us but was isolated and out of view from everyone else. The next task was to collect enough firewood for four days and nights. Then tobacco ties were made. These were pinches of tobacco wrapped in small pieces of cloth that would be tied to four painted posts at the edge of the circle. The posts represented the four major directions, the ties each represented a different prayer where one could make as few or as many as they wished.

Then meals were skipped. First day, breakfast. Second day, lunch. And on the third and last day it was a long sweat lodge ceremony instead of dinner. The next morning it was get up before sunrise and do another sweat lodge, after which we were taken up the hill to our separate sites, one by one. At the site I had chosen I stripped down to my shorts while Two Birds conducted a special pipe ceremony. Then he gave me a wooden match to light a fire in the small fire pit I had made in the center of my circle. That done, he clearly defined the circle on the ground by sprinkling corn meal in two narrow bands around the small area I was in, one yellow, the other blue, said, "Good Luck" and walked off.

It seemed simple enough. Now all I had to do was to stay there inside the circle for as long as possible, hopefully for four days and nights. But there was on major complication.

It was fall, we were at an altitude of almost eight thousand feet and there had been a thick layer of frost on the windshields of our cars the night before. Furthermore, we didn't have any extra matches to relight the fire with if it went out. Therefore, if the fire went out, the quest was over. Mine almost was on the second night when I dozed off but wakened just in time to nurse a few glowing coals back to life with some dried grass, small twigs and lots of huffing and puffing. As for the experience itself, it is impossible to define clearly but the ritual of pipe ceremonies and sweat lodges helped put it a category of it's own. Symbolism, strong words, gestures and energy, can be a powerful thing. Corn meal sprinkled on the ground was more than just a circle. It became an invisible, psychological wall that surrounded and protected me, reaching to the sky as time became warped and wrapped around itself, making it feel like I could have just sat there forever, looking out at the world, no hunger, no thirst, no wants or needs, just a feeling of peace and tranquility to drift away in. And then it was over. Down off the mountain and into the shower, no grand, prophetic vision having been given but a changed person nonetheless.

CAROL AND ROY

Prior to this, back in the early days when I was newly arrived in the area, Dee and I went to someone's house to hear a Hopi Indian talk. He was there to ask for donations. Not for money, however. He wanted large plastic pails instead. Ones with lids on them that could be sealed so that grains and other food stuffs could be stored in them in preparation for the worst that was yet to come. The reason for that comes back to a large rock that stands alone in a wayside parking area up on the mesa in Hopiland near Old Ariabi which has the essence of the Hopi Prophecy inscribed on it. Days long if told orally and far too long to attempt in writing, one aspect of it predicts the apocalyptic path mankind was on with its own "end times" equivalent. First there would be the "Purification" when the evil ones would be swept away. Some of the old traditional elders also believed that certain members of their tribe actually had been endowed with the power to set the entire thing in motion. It was with a special ritualistic dance all its own, something with enormous implications.

Was such a thing possible? Was the fate of the entire world in the hands of a few Native Americans who lived up on a reservation in northern Arizona? Such a conclusion would be hard to accept. On the other hand, there were times when one had to wonder about such things. Like the summer I was up there and was able to watch the Rain Dance. Special costumes for the occasion, drums, rattles, chanting and distinctive steps to the dance. Not a cloud in the sky, it hadn't rained in months. But then, after the ritualistic ceremony was over and I got in my car to go home, the sky turned dark, the lightning flashed and the downpour began. For those who have seen it, it's hard to believe that it just some grand coincidence. And as for coincidence, what about this man who we had come to hear speak. As it turned out he, Roy, a short, middle aged man of slight build, who easily passed as a Hopi, wasn't Hopi at all. He was Indonesian, instead, and what brought him to Hopiland might also be considered to be more than just coincidence.

Roy had been living in Los Angeles in the late nineteen eighties and somehow got caught up in the environmental activism movement of the time and walked clear across the United States in a protest march with Mahatma Gandhi's grandson to Washington DC. There, when the demonstration was over, he met a woman with an old van who offered him a ride as far as Hopi Land on the way home.

Living there was an elderly old traditional Hopi in his nineties named Titus. Titus had lived on several acres of land west of Old Aribbi which he grew hand planted corn on. All was fine until some white man gave him a tractor to cultivate with. Not such a good idea on hilly terrain, the tractor tipped over one day, broke several bones and did other crushing damage to Titus's body. By the time Roy coincidentally arrived, Titus had been moved to his daughter's house in town to mend but was near death instead. Somehow Roy, who had been a physical therapist back in LA, found this out and started taking care of the old man, all in exchange for a place to stay.

Eventually, after several months of treatment, old Titus got his strength back and was able to function again. And that was about the time when I first met Roy who had stayed on in Hopiland and lived with old Titus in a little shack out on Titus's land. At this point Roy and I became friends of a sort and one day I had the honor of meeting old Titus in person when he actually walked into my house in Sedona for a visit. He used a cane and was a little slow physically but there was still a strong life force glowing in his eyes and it was obvious that his mind was clear and sharp, even though I couldn't speak his language.

Shortly after that I made several trips up to the reservation, helped plant corn with a planting stick, met a lot of the natives, was allowed to attend several ceremonial dances and met other traditional Hopi who were having serious issues with the Federal Bureau of Indian Affairs. I also helped Roy with a small newsletter he started called, Hopi and Planetary Friends. At the same time I still had that twenty year old, falling apart Ford van which had technically cost me a little over seventy thousand dollars while the only thing Roy could afford to drive was a, basically unsafe, battered old Toyota compact car so I overhauled the engine in the van and gave the vehicle to him. It was an appropriate thing to do because old Titus loved to ride around the country side and the two of them used the vehicle to explore all the back roads of northern Arizona until Titus finally died in his late nineties. They even used it to go to New Mexico in, where they had the good fortune to meet the Dali Lama who was there on a visit.

The other thing Roy did was to come down to Sedona on occasion and go hiking in the canyons. One of these was Sycamore and that is where he met a woman named Carol who he thought was camping out down there. Well, that sounded like an interesting individual, I decided at the time, a woman brave enough to be living in the wild all alone. That was someone I would like to meet.

With that in mind, I drove out to the canyon and hiked in about a mile. There I climbed up on a big rock alongside the trail and waited. Another coincidence or not, call it what you want, but within ten minutes here came a woman with a day pack on. When she was near enough, I called out to her. Her first reaction was fear. She thought that I might be from the Forest Service. The camping limit was two weeks and by then she had been down there over four months, fully expecting to be evicted. Mentioning Roy's name helped, however, although she had only met him once and very briefly. Regardless, we quickly established a connection and she told me she was hiking into Cottonwood to buy honey and rice. Not such a long hike, she said. Only twelve miles on top of the four she had already made to get where I was. But, after we talked a bit and she checked me out, she accepted my offer of a ride.

I thought Carol's story was very unique. Approximately fifty, five foot five and very physically fit, she had been adopted by a Southern Baptist minister and his wife when she was little. The minister was extremely strict, overbearing and righteous, however, and she had moved out at sixteen to go her own way, eventually as a school teacher. At any rate, five months before I had met her she had been reading a travel magazine which had a one paragraph mention of Sycamore Canyon in it and she knew immediately that was where she wanted to go. With that, she read through a stack of survival books, got in her old Mustang and drove to Cottonwood. There she sold the car, bought a tent and camping gear and hitched a ride out to the canyon. Then she hiked about five miles in to where there were spring fed pools of drinkable water and learned to supplement her diet of honey and rice with cattail roots, manzanita berries and other edible plant life. By the time I had met her she had lived in the tent, a couple of different caves and in an old Indian ruin, all alone without a firearm or other protection all those months, met a mountain lion on the trail and more.

I didn't see a lot of her after that because she liked the solitude of the canyon but she did knock on my door once in a while. When she did I would let her use the shower. Then we would go into town, have breakfast and talk a lot. After that I would lend her as many paper back books as she could carry and give her a ride out to the canyon where she said goodbye for a week or two. I soon began to worry, however, because over a month had gone by without seeing her. Then, another coincidence. I was going down the highway in my old truck when I saw someone walking along side the road. It was a woman. And then, closer, there was Carol with her small day pack on.

Turning around, I drove her into Cottonwood where she had been headed, and we talked. The Forest Service had finally caught up to her and banned her from the canyon. Somehow she had then connected with some local artists and was now living in a tent on their property where she cleaned house and modeled. This lasted for about three months. Then I found that she had moved into Sedona, was living in a minute sized little trailer in someone's back yard and working in the C-market. Again we talked and had breakfast together once in a while. Then, late in the year, she asked me for a favor. Would I drive her up Oak Creek Canyon for her next adventure.

Somewhere about twelve miles up the road she said to pull over. By then it was nearing evening and it had started to snow. I asked her if she really wanted to do this and she said, definitely, so we got out. I opened the trunk when she had stowed her immense back pack and pulled it out. I could hardly lift it. She, however, easily slung it up on her back, buckled the strap around her waist, said goodbye and disappeared into the falling snow by climbing up the side of a steep slope into the trees.

Again, several months went by until I found her back working in the C-market because, once more, she needed the money. This time to buy a new tent and clothing. One winter night she had built a fire outside her tent to warm up with before crawling into her sleeping bag. Then, when it was almost out, she went to look for more wood. While she was searching, the wind gusted heavily, blew the remainder of her fire into the tent where her clothes and supplies were and destroyed it all, thus the need for money. That soon accomplished, she had a new destination in mind. Escalante.

Esaclante was a small town in southern Utah. It was also a river that flowed into Lake Powell. And a deep, extraordinarily beautiful canyon of red rocks and boulders. She told me that was her ultimate goal and then, before I got the chance to see her again, she was gone, never to reappear. That was several years ago now, but I still think of her from time to time, surrounded by her self contained, larger mystery. And I can still see her sometimes, sitting by herself, staring into the fire. Or looking up at the stars on this, her personal quest. And off in the distance, the coyote howls a deeper message before my vision ends. I think she found her final peace up there, somewhere in that immense wilderness, alone with herself in the night, out on the edge of nowhere.

As for the man Roy, who made knowing her possible, I have no idea but it's highly probable that his last resting place may be under one of the mounds on the back side of the hill on Hopiland, having found his own destiny alongside old Titus who is also buried there, my only regret being that I never thanked him for leading me to Carol, one of those people who left me with a lot of unconventional things to think about, realizing how much I would have missed if I hadn't sought her out.

THE DISAPPEARANCE
Unknown to me at the time, there was also another woman who had moved to Sedona named Midge. Midge shared a rental house with a woman named Gina and a Yaqui Indian named Louiss who was a jeep driving tour guide. Midge worked in the Tee Shirt Factory gift shop

across the street from the Talaqapaque shopping center while Gina was the sexy voice on the other end of a 900 number, so much a minute phone call. Gina was instant chemistry when we met but drugs had already stolen her soul and that was the end of that so we return to Midge. Midge worked evenings until the night she failed to come home. A few days later Louiss found her little red pickup truck hidden in the trees out by Fay Canyon and called the police but there were no clues as to what might have happened. Then the stories began. Some of them were rather bizarre but none so strange as the one which might have been the truth, even though the entire thing is still cloaked in unsolved mystery over twenty years later. That story began with my friend Dee.

Dee stopped for breakfast at a coffee shop when coming into town a few days after Midge had disappeared and ended up sitting near two women talking about the event. A mother and daughter, whom Dee introduced herself to. They had been attending the Edgar Cayce Institute in Phoenix when the daughter suddenly felt compelled to come to Sedona and they had spent the previous day there riding around in a hired jeep with a driver. Regardless of never having been to Sedona before, the daughter was able to accurately describe where they wanted to go and they soon ended up out by Fay Canyon, right where Midge's truck had been found. They stopped there for a while then had the driver take them back across the road to an open area at the base of Doe Mountain. Here they got out and walked around before moving on. Eventually they made their way up the hill to Jerome and felt that is where it all began and ended.

At the time it was a known fact that their was an enclave of devil worshipers in the area and one of the leaders lived in Jerome. Interestingly, the psychic daughter was able to pick up on all this and was even able to describe which building this man worked in and the place where several of them lived together in an old building. She also felt that one of their members was a man on the Sedona police force and that any investigation would dead end there, which it eventually did. As for what actually happened on that fateful night, her description went like this.

Midge had been targeted. She had purposely been kidnapped and done away with in a ceremonial ritual late at night out there in that open area by Doe Mountain, the victim of of a dozen devil worshiping, insane individuals. Then she had been decapitated, her body taken up to Jerome and dumped down an old mine shaft. An extreme story perhaps but a week later someone found Midge's backpack where it had been thrown out along the forest road leading from the site to Jerome while several years later a woman's skull was found on a nearby ranch. But that wasn't supposed to be the end of it. According to the psychic daughter, the next victim had already been selected. This woman was described as working somewhere in uptown Sedona in a second floor office and had something to do with a jeep tour company, along with a few more details.

Needless to say, Dee called me and told me the entire story. I, in turn, went over to see Two Birds, who I knew fairly well by then, and related it to him.

"Goddamnit," he said in a loud voice when I got to the part about the next victim. "Them sons a bitches. That's my woman," he said with fire in his eyes.

I guess I was stunned at the time because when I told him, I had no idea where his girlfriend Cheryl worked or what she did but it was all very accurate. Then I told him about Jerome.

With that he went into the kitchen, opened a drawer

and came back with a immense military issue forty five automatic hand gun which he tucked under his belt.

"Cheryl has the car," he said. "Drive me up to Jerome."

Well, there it was, the building exactly as described by the psychic young woman, an outside door leading to an inside stairway to the second floor. Up the stairs, through another door into an open area with a long counter facing the door and behind it two men working in an archival site with old books and documents, the one also fitting the given description. Two Birds walked up to the counter and motioned them over. Then he took out his big forty five, laid it on the counter with his finger on the trigger and told them in a very clear voice that what they were thinking of doing next was not going to happen or he would be back in a much more serious frame of mind.

Weeks went by without incident after that as he watched out for Cheryl with diligence. No one in Jerome called the cops either, as might have happened if he had threatened the wrong people, and life settled down into a more quiet time. I had also moved out to Rimrock by then but drove into Sedona on an almost daily basis to have breakfast with Two Birds and talk. One day he told me he was no longer living with Cheryl. Cheryl had gotten pregnant, hadn't told him about it, went to California for a week, had an abortion, then came home and shared the news with him. Then she left town so, either way, Two Birds didn't have to worry about her safety anymore.

Upset as he was, however, his despair didn't last long. A newly divorced woman named Terra had come to town and seemed a much better companion for him. Eventually they got married in Native American terms and moved to New Mexico. Before that happened, however, Two Birds and I spent a lot of time talking about philosophy and religion and, having a newly acquired copy of a document called the Talmud Jmmanuel, I offered to lend it to him. It was claimed to have been a translation of the Bible before the Christians edited and changed it, which he took home and read. Then everything took on a very strange twist. With nothing to be gained from it and everything to lose, Two Birds story went like this.

A few days after having read the Talmud an oddly dressed man came up to him in the coffee shop on a day when I wasn't there, sat down, looked him over and asked if he had read the document. Yes, and so what and who the hell are you and how the hell do you know I even had it, Two Birds had asked, a bit surprised and wondering what I might have set him up for.

The man then asked him if he had a car and when told he did, the man wanted Two Birds to drive him somewhere because there was something he needed to see and some people he needed to meet. So, curious individual that he was, he finished his breakfast, got in the car and followed directions, determined to get some answers. That took them out to one of the canyons where they stopped and walked back into a secluded clearing in the woods, and then, about an hour later I got a very angry, demanding phone call from Two Birds. Where the hell did I live and how did he get to my house? Then, when he arrived, he was in an extremely agitated and fearful state. A man who had been in heavy combat in the war, sweating profusely, as if frightened to death. Without telling me what happened, he got out his ceremonial, red stone pipe, filled it with tobacco, lit it and proceeded to do a pipe ceremony right there in my front yard. Then, when it was over, and without a word, he handed me the pipe. Not understanding one bit of it, I guessed I was supposed to smoke it too so I took a few puffs and handed it back, whereupon he relaxed a little and started to talk. Much later he told me that if I hadn't smoked with him he would have left but since I did, he felt I was to be trusted.

And where had I gotten that damned document? he wanted to know.

Switzerland, I replied and then he relayed his story. There had been a shiny round craft sitting in that clearing along with two other people, a man and a woman and they were there to tell him that, among other things, he had a new mission in life. Unusual as it might sound, he was supposed to acquire seven women-wives, as they called them, and have a child with each one of them, all of which would be girls. Christ wasn't returning to earth after two thousand years as a man. This time Jmmanual would be an Jmmanuella, a woman. There would be no wise men showing up either, no indications of a divine being. She would come quietly and only later in her life would she become a person with a message. Not a holy one shrouded in religious piousness but a practical one instead, with words to live by.

Pretty damned grandiose, I thought at first. Had agent orange also dissolved part of his brain, I wondered. What else had he been smoking besides Lucky Strikes and his pipe? And if any of it was in any way true, where did I fit in? What kind of messenger was I, giving him that document and how would anyone else have known about it to begin with? But what was I supposed to say? I had no idea how it all could have happened. And if he was telling the truth, then someone was using me to get to him and the thought of that made me very upset too. But was he telling the truth, this war veteran standing there in front of me, completely shaken, upset, confused and more, almost frightened to death. No one could have faked that. And what, if anything, would there have been to be gained by doing so anyway? In all the time I had known Two Birds he had never told me any personal war stories, discussed his accomplishments or even hinted at his own self importance. He also had a deep respect for other people, was not racist or sexist and basically modest about his own importance. So, all in all, damned if the entire episode hasn't left me as confused as he seemed to have been at the time.

Well, it was the first and only time we ever talked about it but we stayed friends regardless, even though he soon moved to New Mexico with the new woman in his life. He also returned to give a weekend retreat at a friend's house down by the creek and I went to a few more in California which he hosted and was given my Indian name. This was done at a special ceremony for eleven of us. We gathered around a fire in a circle. Twobirds filled his pipe with tobacco, did a special ritual then walked around behind us. Here he stopped behind each person, thought a while, then named us one by one. Why he came up with what he did for me, I have no idea but I was pleased to be something besides another Running Elk, Standing Bull or other more ordinary creature. He-Who-Looks-Into-The-Sun has broader connotations and contains an element of mystery I found pleasing and so much for that.

After that he went to Australia on a speaking tour and came back with a red head who moved in with him and Terra in New Mexico. Other speaking engagements gave him two more woman, plus he also picked up a couple of guys who were to be apprentices, learning the native ways of sweat lodges and ceremony and that is where I went to participate in my vision quest. As for Two Birds himself, except for all these extra women in his life, he seemed as normal, logical and astute as ever. Because of the distance, however, I saw less and less of him after that and then finally got a letter from Idaho where they had all moved to work on a reservation. Then again, another letter two years years later still, from Alamogordo, New Mexico.

Conveniently enough at the time, I had just planned a trip to Virginia to see some family and was able to stop and see him en route and spend the night.

There were four women and three babies in the house this time, all girls of course, but we talked of other things and other times instead. I told him I had written a book based on life in Sedona, had endowed him with a lot of magical powers and made him one of the main characters which made him chuckle. Then I gave him a copy of the manuscript and told him that if he wanted me to change any of it, he should let me know. Well, I never heard from him again, nor did I think I would because agent orange was now taking its toll in a more serious way. He could hardly walk for one thing because bone cancer was destroying his knees. It had also progressed and a portion of his face had been carved away too. But I never once ever doubted the sincerity of our friendship and what else mattered?

I know he is long gone now, it's been several years, but when I think of him I think of another story he once told me and I see him standing on the beach in Coronado, down by San Diego. The only person there and simply because he felt like doing it, he began conducting a pipe ceremony. Then the seagulls started arriving. More came, and even more until they completely surrounded him on the sand, an immense flock of white birds listening to his words. It always reminds me of the time my friend Dee and I were up on a hill and the ravens came to surround us too, also in large numbers. White birds for him, black birds for us. Ravens are wise, what are seagulls? Doesn't matter, this is still how I choose to remember him best while I also still try to pay attention to what goes on along the periphery of daily events, wondering if some special young women, one of his daughters, will somehow appear on the scene with a different life perspective. But will she?

Is it all just too damned bizarre? And then too, what would others think if I told them I had had a UFO encounter of my own?

For one six month period I lived in a house that sat alone out on a ridge below the town of Jerome.. With that in mind, imagine me sitting there one evening just at dusk, looking out over the valley below .... when, down over the house came this glowing, spherical object about eighteen inches in diameter that followed the terrain and disappeared over the crest of the hill, headed in a straight line path. Then, about a week later, I was driving along a road down in the valley one night when the same object literally flew across the road right in front of my truck, about the same distance off the ground and headed in what would be the same direction as before, when it went over the front yard of my house.

The first time I saw this object, the reaction was rather odd. On the one hand, I saw it very clearly. On the other, such an object is so out of context and in such contradiction to the normal world that my mind seemed to block me from acknowledging the event completely. The second time, however, confirmed the first sighting and forced me to think about it a little more openly, especially from a technical viewpoint since, career wise I had spent many years working as a "rocket scientist. Assuming that I actually saw what I thought I did, what could I then say about that while still retaining as much skepticism as possible? The conclusions that can be drawn are immense. Here are some of them.

The object obviously had an on-board power source that could propel it forward and defy the force of gravity. It did not rise up like a glowing bubble of gas and get carried along by the wind but was also intelligently guided and had a specific course to follow with a specific end location to return to, either pre programmed or remotely controlled by some form of intelligence. It was, therefore, there for a reason. It had a purpose and was on a mission, limited as that might be. Most likely a probe or telemetry disk, gathering data. Either recording it or transmitting it back to a control station. But to what end? Did the fact that I saw it coming down the hill from Jerome have any specific significance? What was so special about an old mining town clinging to the side of a mountain? Was it the geology or the people who lived there? Or was it just a limited part of a much broader, far more extensive survey that was under way? After all, lots of other people claim to have seen similar things, notably in the Sedona area for one. And up on the Hopi Reservation for another. Old Titus, the Hopi elder I met when I first came to Sedona, drew a picture of a UFO that had landed in his corn field and other Hopi stated that they saw such craft all the time. So what about that, along with all the multi millions of people world wide who claim such experiences? Ones which imply the existence of highly advanced extra terrestrial life. At least technologically, having knowledge that earth science has yet to discover.

Unfortunately, however, it is a subject area most intelligent people try hard to avoid because it is so muddied and distorted by attention starved, crazy people that confuse the entire issue. It is also philosophically disruptive for the more rational. How does one fold the idea of visitors from outer space, and all that that implies, into what they have been led to believe about life and its purpose? It seems difficult at best so instead of trying to debate the issue, let me tell you about another Native American experience I had at the time, one that I also consider to be of significance. The Sun Dance.

SUN DANCE
Another friend at the time was a Yaqui indian named

Mario. One day he showed me the scars on his chest. These came from having had his skin pierced on both sides where wooden pegs had been inserted so he could engage in the Sun Dance. The previous summer he had gone to the Rosebud reservation in South Dakota and did just that and he would soon be off to do it again but this time I was invited. At this time the White man was not only permitted to come and witness the event on this particular reservation, he, or she, could also participate in the ritual itself if they were willing to make a four year commitment for doing so. But why was he doing this? I asked. To help conquer his fear of dying, he said and with that I drove north that summer to see what he had gotten involved in first hand.

Fear can become a driving force that compels people to behave in irrational ways and it was out of fear that the federal government banned ceremonial dances and rituals by Native Americans across the entire country very early in it's history. Fear and righteousness also led to Indian children being abducted from their homes and sent to the white man's schools in an attempt to destroy native languages and culture. It went on from there, a shameful period in American history and it wasn't until 1978 that the American Indian Religious Freedom act was passed but by then much damage had been done. So many generations had gone by by that the detailed steps and procedures for conducting the Sun Dance, for one, had been largely forgotten and had to be pieced back together. But it was and for me, certain parts of it became a spiritual experience that is hard to forget. One of these was the tree that becomes the center pole in the arena to which all the dancer's ropes are tied.

This tree was selected the previous summer and every day for a year someone went to it out in the woods, sprinkled tobacco around it and conducted an appropriate ceremony. Then, on the day before the dancing began, the tree was cut down. But hardly in an ordinary way. A large group of men went out to the site and caught it as it fell so that its branches never touched the ground. Then it was placed on a truck and taken to the dance arena where it was placed on a carpet of wild sage so that again it wouldn't be on the bare ground. Then it was left there to die over night. And that was the unusual part.

After most of the people had dispersed I stood there and watched the tree for a long time and somehow it seemed that I was picking up on what it was going through. For one thing it knew it was dying and it was very sad as its life force began to dwindle and drift away. It had loved being a tree out in the woods with those other trees, loved the sun, the rain and the wind, the birds that sat on its branches and even the winter snow and it was sad to be leaving that behind but also honored at the sacrifice it had been asked to make. I don't know if anyone else sensed what I did or felt what I felt but I did see a couple of tribal men watching it in silence too, along with one native woman who stood there for a long time before dropping her head and walking away. As for me personally, now that I have experienced that, I find myself looking at trees and plants with much more reverence than before and sometimes even find myself apologizing to weeds that decide to grow in my yard before pulling them up. I try not to step on ants anymore, either and often catch crickets, bees and bugs that find their way into the house and put them outside with a message to please not invade my space. Having been stung by too many scorpions, however, I show them no mercy whatsoever. I also think I'd rather get bitten by a mountain line than a black widow spider or a rattlesnake. But, back to the dance.

The next morning at sun up, the dancers, already having had a round in the sweat lodge, tied their individual ropes high up on the tree trunk and the tree, which I thought was still somewhat alive, was lifted upright and set in place. Then the dancers hooked themselves to their ropes, the drum beat started and the ceremony began. The specifics are not important. What is, is the challenge and change it brings to the participant. Even the onlooker. Additionally, the Chief also spoke several times during the days long ceremony about a variety of things relating to the challenges his people faced. One of the major ones was the ongoing prejudice and harassment from the outside world, including local and state police. Technically, the reservations are considered to be sovereign nations but ultimately they fall under the jurisdiction of the Federal Bureau of Indian Affairs, the BIA as it is referred to, a grossly mismanaged, convoluted, essentially corrupt bureaucratic nightmare that is widely despised by those who are forced to live under its often arbitrary and twisted rules, regulations and policy decisions.

Beyond that on the more immediate level, the reservation was faced with very high unemployment and poverty. There was still alcoholism and a rift of other social problems. These, the chief stated, were all largely traceable back to one particular root cause. By refusing to grant the Indian the equal rights and recognition given to any other ethnic group and treating him like a savage, the "White man" had robbed the Native, not only of his land and heritage, but of his dignity and very identity. The Sun Dance, along with other native ceremonies, was one way of helping the individual gain some of it back and from what I saw for those who dedicated themselves to it, it seemed to work. Completing the dance was not only a test of endurance but also an expression of individuality and something to take pride in that would carry over into other life situations. I know it worked for my friend Mario because the change was more than evident after his four year commitment. So dedicated was he that he went back again for another four years.

As for the Sun Dance ceremony I attended, it also had another ancient ceremony folded in with it at the end. The Tribal Chief of the time passed on his position to his successor in a costumed ritual, full eagle feathered headdress and all, with only one thing lacking, both during the Sun Dance and this ceremony. That was some proper drums. The drummers at both of these events all pounded on a large, commercially made, bass drum that might have once belonged to a high school band which I found disturbing and out of character. There was nothing I could do about that but I did have one smaller, hand held drum with me that I had made for myself so I could add my own sounds to the beat around the fire pit at the drumming circles up on the hill in Sedona. Actually I made many of them before I stopped, probably a hundred in all. I sold a few but gave most of them away. And then, there I was, privileged to give away one more. This one to the Lakota Chief at the Sun Dance up on the reservation in South Dakota.

I started making drums because most of those available in the shops were flimsy, poorly made and unattractive, while the good ones were ridiculously expensive so I experimented and made my own, ones that were unique at the time. Instead of bending a thin piece of wood around in a circle and covering it with deer or cowhide, most of my drums were sturdy eight sided creations covered with elk. A very different shape at the time which other people soon began to copy. That part didn't matter. The pleasure was in being able to give so many away to people I thought were special, like the Chief.

Then the entire days long event was over and after a side trip I was back in the Sedona area, still living in my truck. Since that time, however, there have been council meetings attended by tribal leaders from around the world and in 2003 it was decided to totally ban non natives from such events as the Sun Dance. Rightfully so, I believe, because the white man was also trying to steal and reprocate some of these rituals, for profit, of course. The self appointed gurus and motivational shamans of the western world had found that it was very profitable to copy Native American ceremonies and charge fees for participation. Unfortunately, such a focus often leads to serious mistakes and suddenly there was a rash of white people suffering from third degree burns on the bottom of their feet from attempting the Fire Walk while many others were dying from suffocation in sweat lodges in attempts that were only designed to feed the egos and wallets of the promoters. Banning the non natives from indigenous ceremonies will not stop that kind of abuse, however, but it was a strong declaration nonetheless that seems to deserve respect.

And then there is the travesty of Mount Rushmore and the proud assertion of Crazy Horse Mountain. Mt. Rushmore was designed as a tourist attraction that honors American presidents while Crazy Horse Mountain honors the man who is said to be the real patriot of the Sioux tribe. The man who fought against the land grabbing federal government which set out to destroy the Native American way of life in the Dakotas, a man ultimately murdered by the U. S. Military.

When I left the Sun Dance I diverted and re visited these two sites after some forty years near Custer, South

Dakota. Only seventeen miles apart, Mount Rushmore is a National Monument on land originally stolen from the natives while Crazy Horse is on what is still private indian land. While Mt. Rushmore may be labeled an artistic accomplishment when considered separately, it becomes an abomination and an affront when its location is taken into account and a declaration of dominance over a once proud group of people. Tourist attraction that it is, plain and simple in my opinion, it just does not belong there. Back east, perhaps, but not where it is and if Crazy Horse Memorial wasn't in progress and I were Native American I might consider blowing Rushmore up. Ultimately, it looks like the natives will prevail, however, because the Crazy Horse sculpture is not only bolder in concept, it already dwarfs Rushmore, both conceptually and dimensionally. Not only is the head of Crazy Horse forty percent larger than the Rushmore heads of the presidents, the final work will include him full body on horseback, making the entirety of the statue orders of magnitude greater in size and accomplishment, dwarfing the message and importance of Rushmore, something long overdue.

TURN HERE

Later that year, still living in my old truck, I drove to Oregon to see my brother. Then I drove east to see my sister in Denver, always a most delightful individual full of enthusiasm and from there went on to Wisconsin to look up an old friend, and lastly headed south, sleeping in my vehicle along the way, destination Florida. One of my reasons for wanting to go there was to swim with the dolphins which was claimed by some to be a magical experience all its own. I didn't want it to be in an oversized pool, however, but in open water. So, with that as my goal, there I was at last, headed south down Highway One, destination, Key West, no idea as to how to bring it about. But I never worry about such things because, invariably, they always seem to take care of themselves. Like this one eventually did in it's own unexpected way where on a nice sunny morning on Key Largo, an odd chain of events began to unfold.

Going down the four lane highway, I was approaching a dirt road that went off to the right when a voice of sorts told me to turn in there. I had no idea where it led but it was through an area of high bushes, small trees and other thick growth that prevented me from seeing what might be back in there. I continued anyway, eventually coming to a large clearing and a rather large house. I stopped, got out and waited, having the clear feeling that no one was there. Then, looking around, I saw an elevated wooden walkway that led off through a wet area full of tall rushes and marsh grass. I followed it and there at the end was a huge structure made entirely of chicken wire fencing where several people were inside hurrying around. Outside, standing there, this woman looked at me when I was close enough and said, "You're right on time. Come on, get busy."

I nodded and went inside where it was immediately obvious what everyone was trying to do. They were catching wild pelicans. So I caught wild pelicans that were then stuffed into small, transportable cages. They weren't normal pelicans, however. They had all been injured in some way. Missing feet, broken wings, other things and this was a rescue station and the reason we were catching them was because a hurricane was coming and if they were left in the bigger structure the high winds would blow then around and injure them even further. As a result, once captured they were to be placed in the basement of the house I saw earlier, until the storm was over. That accomplished, I was ready to get back on the road when the same woman as before asked if I had heard about the baby whale.

"No, what whale?" I asked and then, there I was, headed back to the north. A few miles away there was a wide channel that flowed across the island from east to west. In that channel was another group of people trying to save the life of a baby sperm whale. It had been found beached on the shore farther up the coast and brought there for this rescue group to manage. Just an infant about ten feet long, it had to be feed, burped, exercised and kept afloat. There were five or six swimmers in the water around the clock to help do that and their intent was to ride out the storm wearing football helmets to protect them while they did. Feeding was done through a large plastic hose stuck in its mouth through which gallons of human baby formula were poured on a regular basis. Burping was accomplished by rolling it over in the water a few times after feeding. Exercise was forced by manually moving its flippers and tail back and forth and I took turns with some of the rescuers in the water.

By morning the hurricane had skipped on past, however, and the baby whale had made some progress so I told the group leader I was leaving. He asked where I was going.

"Key West," I said. "I want to swim with the dolphins in open water," and with that he found a scrap of paper and wrote down the name and phone number of a woman in Key West. She, as it turned out, just happened to own a boat. So, there I was a few hours later, out in the open water being dragged by a rope, surrounded by a pod of eight or nine dolphins. But was it a magical experience? No, not exactly. Catching wild pelicans and swimming with a baby whale had been much more up close and personal.

Regardless, while relatively rare in general, these intuitive experiences do happen, usually related to some specific need of my own that I benefit from directly. But then there are others that are even more difficult to explain, where more critical issue are involved. One such incident that was particularly significant happened back when I was still married to my second wife.

Boating off the California coast as we had done many times before, my then wife and I had spent the day fishing on the far side of Anacapa Island. It was early evening when we came in and we were tired and ready to go home. I was at the controls, just coming around the southern end of the harbor breakwater, ready to head up the channel to the docks when for some unknown reason I felt compelled to ask my wife if she wanted to go down to Port Hueneme which was about a mile south. Why, I had no idea. Remembering the one previous time we had been there years before, there was no reason to repeat the experience. It was just a very small harbor that belonged to the Navy and all it contained was a few old rusting ships. She shrugged her approval anyway and off we went. me beginning to feel some sense of unknown urgency about the whole thing.

Again, however, coming in past the breakwater there, the same old scene as before. A few rusty hulks of ships. Different, however, was the fact that now there was a crowd of people standing on the inner breakwater all shouting and waving frantically, pointing to a place somewhere out in our direction. Obviously serious, we began trying to see what they wanted and where they wanted us to go. Unfortunately the wind was up and the water was very choppy so we could neither make out what they were shouting about or see whatever it was they might be pointing at. Who knew, maybe it was shark. Then finally, and luckily, we saw the problem. A man in the water floating on his back, not moving. At first I was sure he was dead.

Between the wind and the waves it was nearly impossible to get very close without the risk of getting him tangled up in the propeller before I finally managed to lift the poor man aboard. Cold and unconscious, definitely hypothermic, he seemed dead. But then we found a pulse. Back at the helm I got on the radio to the Oxnard harbor master while my wife covered the man with a blanket and massaged him vigorously as we roared back up the coast and down the five mile per hour channel at full speed to where an ambulance was waiting. Still unconscious but still alive, the man left the scene in the emergency vehicle, sirens wailing.

Months later someone knocked on our front door. It was the survivor, who having somehow tracked us down, came to say thanks. He had been fishing from the breakwater and had been swept off the rocks by a large wave. Between the wind, waves and heavy clothes he was wearing, he was unable to swim back to safety. He said for sure he knew he was going to die and at that point had given up. Tragically, he had taken his two small daughters along with him and they were trapped there on shore, watching the entire event unfold. I don't remember the exact number but he told us what his body core temperature had dropped to and it was one of those situation where another five minutes would have given the story an entirely different ending. As for my own personal life story at that time, it was also in transition but if someone had been able to tell me how it would all turn out, I seriously doubt if I would have believed a word of it. And, in that respect, I can think of no other way to tell it except to go back to the real beginning and start with a bit of history.

A BIT OF HISTORY
They came to the United States in the late eighteen

hundreds. Brothers, cousins, friends and acquaintances. They came primarily to avoid a mandatory peacetime draft into the Danish armed services and settled in rural Wisconsin, homesteading land in the area north of Portage. At the time my Grandfather (Soren) built a house on a one hundred sixty acre piece of land and harvested wire grass, a long, durable fibrous material much in demand at the time for use in weaving grass mats, baskets and similar products. It was also the house he died in, along with my Grandmother (Ingeborg), several years before I came along so I never knew them.

My father, born in 1905, was the first of eight children, three boys and five girls, two of which died at birth. When he was old enough to go to school his father took him to the one room school house down the road on horse back and dropped him off. He could not speak English and only remembers standing there when the bell rang, wondering what to do, and because all the others went inside, he followed. All together he received about two years of intermittent schooling, being kept from going most of the time to help on the farm. Ultimately, he left home at fourteen because his father was reported to have been an extremely harsh, hard driving man so he moved into Portage where he worked at the shoe factory until his parents died about three years later.

Long before electric power was available in rural areas my grandfather had somehow put together a system and electrified his own farm. A gas-engine driven generator was located in the basement of the old farmhouse with the exhaust piped to the outside. Perhaps the wind was wrong, maybe there was a leak in the exhaust system, either way it didn't matter because one morning my father's parents were found dead from carbon monoxide poisoning. Fortunately for the rest of his family, it was a two story house where the children all slept upstairs where they were safe and my father, now twenty and the eldest, returned home to take care of his brothers and sisters.

My mother lived on the adjacent farm, one of eight children, six of whom lived. Her parents were Ellsworth and Bessie Thomas and she and my father were married in 1926. In early 1929 the stock market was booming. My parents were doing well on the farm. They had one child and one on the way. In the fall they even bought a new car. But then, on the day I was born, the stock market crashed and the Great Depression began.

The farm was mortgaged and soon foreclosed on by the bank as unemployment multiplied and the economy failed. The new car was also soon given up. At that point we moved about a mile down the road to a rental farm that was only four miles out in the country. Somehow my father was able to regain his job at the shoe factory and for three years walked into town to hold down the job. Then we moved to another smaller farm located just outside the town limits where I began Kindergarten, walking about a mile to school each day. Besides my father still working at the shoe factory, my parents also ran the farms we lived on. There were a few cows to milk, chickens and pigs to feed, corn and hay to harvest. In the summer and fall the kitchen stove was always busy as Mason jars were cleaned, sterilized and filled with home grown vegetables, sealed and placed in the basement for winter food supply along with sacks and sacks of potatoes and baskets of apples. Apples were also sliced and placed on the screens taken off the windows and placed on the roof in the sun to dry. Another major fall task was cutting wood for fuel.

There were no forced air furnaces in the houses we lived in then, either. The source of heat was a pot bellied stove that sat in the dining room. The living rooms were closed off in winter and bedrooms went unheated to conserve fuel, leaving the dining room and kitchen as the only two warm places in the entire house. Long before chain saws, an acre or two of trees had to be manually chopped down with an ax, branches trimmed off and then cut up to be stacked in the woodshed for the winters which could often be long and bitterly cold. There was no indoor plumbing either, which added the additional burden of having to carry water in, a pailful at a time and too bad if you woke up in the middle of a winter night and had to go potty when it was below zero out. There was no electricity in these early houses either, and flashlights hadn't been invented yet which made everything an even bigger ordeal. Later, having been in school for a while and learning about where we lived with respect to the rest of the country and how big it really was always made me wonder why, if they was going to emigrate, why they never picked a place that was farther south and a little warmer.

Back then, however, the world I lived in as a child was very small and limited and finally, when I was in the first grade we moved in to town itself. That house was not only old, but drafty and in poor condition and in the colder days of winter the water pipes would freeze up under the kitchen floor whereupon the floor had to be pulled up and a blowtorch used to thaw them. The house was also directly across the road from the railroad yard and the power company substation. Other than that, my memories of that house are dim except for the fact that money was still very scarce, we kids all wore a lot of handed down clothing and it seemed that my belly was always just a little short of being full.

The next house was in better condition and in a better part of town but still without a furnace so the pot bellied stove still sat in the dining room during the winter, still needing large amounts of wood for fuel as before. But it did have a bathroom with a real bathtub. No water heater though but it was certainly better than having to stand up in a big old pail to get scrubbed down once a week. Fortunately for my father, it was now an easy walk of only four city blocks to the shoe factory where he still worked. My mother also got a part time job as a clerk in the local clothing store but still found time to cook for her four children, tend to a garden out back and do a lot of canning in the fall. My even more resourceful father also rented an acre of land and planted it all in potatoes which were dug up in the fall, sacked and placed in the cellar. He also became very good at repairing and overhauling auto engines and made extra money that way. It was a good skill to have during the war when cars were not being manufactured so cars would end up with Ford parts in Chevies, or whatever else it took to keep them running.

A neighbor friend and he also built themselves each a rowboat and on summer weekends they would camp out by the river, use multiple hooked set lines and come home with enough fish to feed half the neighborhood. Additionally, my mother's father, my living grandfather, would butcher a steer and a couple of hogs in the fall and the meat was shared by family members. There were no deep freezers then, however, so it was another thing that was cooked and canned. My father also built his own table saw, band saw and scroll saw and made furniture for the house and other items to sell or give away and that is where I became his, not always so willing, assistant.

One of the things he made many of was a very intricate, decorative shelf that demanded hours of labor cutting out figures of deer, foxes and hounds and little fences that had dozens of holes in them that had to be individually cut out on the scroll saw. I don't know how old I was at the time but I remember having to stand on an orange crate to operate the saw, so I must have been about ten. One of those summers and still not very old, I was also given the job of painting the two story garage and storage shed out back and if there were other odd jobs that needed doing, I was the one who ended up doing them. Likewise, when summer came and school was out, I was the one who also got sent out to my grandfather's farm to help him, primarily because I was the only one he had any patience for. Sometimes it was a week or two, sometimes longer, one less person to have to feed back home. No indoor plumbing there, no electric lights, the source of heat a wood burning stove in the kitchen. No other kids around within miles, it often got very lonely.

My grandparents rarely spoke to each other, or to me, except as necessary to get all the work done and there were times when she seemed to do more than he. Up before the sun, the cows would be waiting in the barnyard to get milked and she would do almost as many as he, then go back to the house, light a fire in the stove and cook breakfast. After that she feed the chickens, gathered up the eggs, ran the cream separator and worked in the garden. A very big garden that needed planting and weeding and harvesting and led to an immense amount of cooking and canning to put up food for the winter. This is not meant to imply that my grandfather was lazy, however, because he was not.

The farm they lived on was one hundred and sixty acres and primarily a dairy farm with at least twenty cows to attend to. No tractor at the time, the two main crops he planted were corn and hay and all the plowing, discing, dragging, mowing and cultivating were done with horses so there were many long hard days, especially in the spring and fall. They also raised a lot of hogs, ducks, geese and sometimes a few goats. As for my grandfather, I don't think he liked being a farmer and that turned him into the stubborn, difficult, churlish, hard to please and hard to get along with man he could often be and it was his stubbornness which led to his demise when I was twenty two. Somehow he had injured his leg and refused to see a doctor which led to blood poisoning and death at seventy four. After he was gone, I have to say that my grandmother seemed happier in some respects and the last time I saw her she was eighty five and living with and taking care of a younger woman who was only seventy but had Alzheimer and needed constant care. Many things still stand out in memory of my time on their farm but just a few are worthy of note to me.

One was a big black, highly spirited stallion that belonged to a neighbor who couldn't manage the animal. A cowboy would have a put a saddle on it and rode it, bucking and kicking, until it wore itself out and gave up. But not my grandfather. He used his "black snake" instead. The black snake was a ten foot long woven leather whip that was very effective. One snap of it across the rear of most any animal would immediately get it to behave but not this big beautifully, almost wild horse with a mind of its own. So, there they were, out in the yard by the barn, the horse haltered but not liking it very much because every time it would rear up the big whip would snap and leave a welt on its hindquarters which, at first, only made it more determined to break free and get away. So it reared and snorted and flailed the air with it's front hooves, over and over, but each time it did my grandfather would pull its head back down and the big whip would crack and leave another mark on its backside. Round and round they went, the animal and the merciless man, for what seemed to be at least an hour until finally the horse stopped, dropped its head in submission and just stood there, broken spirited, unable to fight any longer.

Another memory is of my own encounters with a wild animal on the farm when I was about ten. At the time I was watching my grandfather mowing hay in the alfalfa field when he scared up a rabbit which I then began to chase. Back and forth we went across the mowed area, me thinking it was a lot of fun. But then, finally, after several long minutes and a lot of chasing, the rabbit just stopped and stood there looking at me. Surprisingly, it didn't run again when I came near and I was able to actually grab it by the ears and pick it up. It didn't fight me either, and try to get away. Instead, I carried it over so I could show it to my grandfather who stopped mowing and took it away from me. Being proud of my accomplishment, all I wanted was to let him see it and then let it go. Instead, he reached in his pocket, took out his big jack-knife and slit the poor creatures throat. Then he slit it down the belly, removed the insides and skinned the poor thing right there in the field, handed it back to me and told me to take it to the house and give it to my grandmother who then cooked it for dinner. Fortunately for me, after it was roasted and cut up, it no longer looked like the thing I had caught earlier and I was actually able to eat a piece or two.

The next thing of importance was learning to drive. The first time for that was in the fall when I was twelve after the Cherry Camp and paper bailing experiences when I was again relegated to the farm. My grandfather had already mowed the hay in one field and had it raked up into long rows, waiting to be put in the barn. For him working alone that meant taking his old flatbed truck down to the field, pitching hay onto it, drive the truck a little father ahead, get out, pitch more on, drive ahead a bit and keep repeating the process again and again, making it an overly difficult job. But now, there I was, so down to the field we went where he stopped the truck at the end of a long row of piled up hay where we got out and he pitched on that small section. then instead of him getting in and pulling ahead, he told me to get it and drive, assuming what, I wasn't sure.

Of course I knew how to drive. I always watched my father when he drove and knew about the clutch, brakes, gas pedal and all the gear positions. I just had never been behind the wheel before, that was all. Pretty jerky at first. Killed the engine a few times but eventually we made it down the row until we had a full load. Then he drove back to the barn , dumped the load and returned to the field where I was again in the drivers seat. A bit scary for me at the time but not half as bad as the time my father told me to take the family car and drive across town by myself to pick up some parts for him when I was only thirteen.

One last experience of some importance regarding my grandfather's farm was the following summer. That year my mother not only sent me out to the farm but also sent my younger brother along with me which seemed to have upset my grandfather quite a bit because he was far grumpier than usual. I believe we were only there four days, or maybe five. Didn't matter. Then they left us alone while they went into town to do some shopping. Once gone, it didn't take us long to make a decision. We hit the road on foot and walked the five miles back home, always hitting the ditch when we heard a car coming so we wouldn't be caught. Again, there we were when my mother got home from her job at the department store, but not a word or a question as to what might have happened. My grandparents never brought the subject up either and no one ever spoke of it. Regardless, even though that ended my having to spend time out on the farm, it didn't seem to affect the relationship with my grandparents long term. Actually, I saw them many times over the years, even introduced them to one of my girl friends later on and would lend a hand once in a while when I visited but never spent another whole night. And now, back to being twelve.

TWELVE

In that time period, if you looked twelve and said you were twelve, you were twelve. And if you were twelve you were old enough to have a paper route, delivering the local news door to door. Therefore, I was twelve in September even though my birthday wasn't until late October and my brother Ted, a year and a half older, passed his paper route on to me. Fortunately, prior to that I had saved enough to buy a used bicycle, five dollars, so I didn't have to walk the two plus miles the route encompassed. Not so bad during the fall except there was no time after school for other activities. But the winters were horrific. After all these years I can still remember pushing my bike through the falling snow whipped by the wind that quickly got too deep to ride through. That and the eeerie sound the wind made as it whistled through the spokes of the bike wheels while darkness fell long before I finally got home, always chilled to the core, hoping that I got there before dinner was served so there was something hot to eat. After dinner it was homework time if there was any. No TV, however. That hadn't been invented yet either.

There old magazines to read, though. We had an erector set, checkers and dominoes and bedtime was always nine o'clock for us kids. No bed time hugs, though. No hugs ever, even when things weren't going well or you weren't feeling very well. Just go to bed so you could get up in the morning and do it all over again. Our bedrooms were in the unheated upstairs and on really cold night I would climb in with my clothes on and slowly undress, one item at a time as the bed warmed up. That was the way it was, it was something I was unable to question because at the time there was no reference to compare it to in order to formulate any questions to ask. It was just something that was expected and endured.

All that was bad enough but the most agonizing part of the paper route was collection. Being very shy at the time, it was extremely difficult for me to knock on doors and ask for money. Some paid it willingly but others would try to put you off. Some didn't even bother to answer the door even though it was obvious they were home and sadly to say, I was way behind in collecting. Unfortunately, that didn't seem to matter to anyone except me. All the newspaper cared about was some minimum amount and the rest belonged to the carriers, us kids. No one in the office every looked at the route book or seemed concerned if people didn't pay. Nor did my parents. They never asked about such things either. As a result I struggled through it, collecting just enough to have a dollar or two extra for myself every week, most of which went for candy, something we rarely got unless we were able to buy it for ourselves and I think it was the chocolate I was able to buy that kept me going through that part of life. Finally, thank god, spring came and I decided I wasn't going to do that anymore. But I didn't officially quit. I just left my route book laying on the counter in the newspaper office and never went back and again, not a word or question from anyone.

My mother figured it out quickly enough, however, and as soon as school was out she took me to my grandfather's farm and dropped me off where I stayed until my grandfather in turn, dropped me off at home a couple of weeks later. Then my mother found another opportunity to have one less child to feed. Still only twelve, she thought she was doing the right thing by shipping me off to Cherry Camp with a total stranger who obviously had some strong recruiting skills. I shared this pleasure with two neighbor boys and a half dozen others he had collected elsewhere in town, most of them a little older. A last minute thing. My mother found out about this grand opportunity around noon and an hour later I was on the way. Nor was I sent off with a bag full of fresh clothes and a box of sandwiches. The two neighbor kids and I went with what we had on our backs and the food we had in our bellies, taking our chances that it would somehow turn out okay. Unlike me, these two brothers were there under more dire circumstances. Their father had driven his car into the garage one night, shut the door and let the engine run and no one found him until it was too late. Seven children in all, it was an even more difficult time for them and we started out with high expectations.

Unfortunately, Cherry Camp wasn't exactly play time for rich kids. You went there to work. Back then child labor laws weren't even thought of, let alone passed and before the summer I had my own social security card, something not issued at birth but earned with a legitimate job.

We didn't ride up to this work camp in a limo either. It was on the back of an open truck and in those days on those roads, two hundred miles was an extremely long ride, breathing exhaust fumes and hanging on for dear life on the corners. It began in south central Wisconsin where we lived and ended out near the end of the Green Bay Peninsula, north of Sturgeon Bay. And when we finally arrived it became clear that camp was not the Hilton. Nor a comfy dormitory. Camp was a run down old barracks with triple decker bunks and a dilapidated mess hall. One small box of cereal in the morning for breakfast, a baloney sandwich for lunch and goulash for dinner, a single sheet and an old army blanket for the night.

As for the work, cherries were picked off the trees, one by one. Doing it this way took a lot of picking to make a pailful and at five cents a pail, it took a long time to gross a dollar. Bad enough but after room and board deductions at the end of the week we found we had netted about fifty cents apiece, which came to something like a penny an hour for all the hard work we had done. Somehow, to the two neighbor kids and myself, that didn't seem to be very much for having had to climb up and down a very tall ladder all day long in the hot sun, gathering blisters and being yelled at over the sound of our stomachs growling with hunger. So, after looking at our half dollars worth of coins and a very brief discussion, we decided to hit the road back home.

Since neither of our families had a telephone, we figured we could get back there before the camp could send a letter declaring our absence, which of course they didn't bother to do anyway. Probably because they didn't have one to begin with. At any rate we were pretty good with our thumbs. The problem was that there just wasn't any through traffic in that part of the world on those old back roads. All of our rides came from some farmer going into town or some other farmer going back home from town and in between we walked. No GPS system, not even a map, we relied on others to keep us going in the right direction. We spent one hungry night sleeping in a cornfield and picked up a few lucky rides the next day. Better still, towards evening when it looked like we might be sleeping in the tall grass alongside the ditch, a kind farmer picked us, let us sit in the kitchen with the rest of his family and share their dinner with them, then turned us loose in his barn to sleep in the hayloft.

The following day a soapless bath in a creek, clothes and all, and once dried out from walking in the sun, two long rides that brought us to within forty miles of our destination. It was getting dark by then but with confident desperation we took our chances and found the local police station. Although nearing its end, the country was still trapped in the Depression. There were homeless, helpless people everywhere and besides we were kids and there was nothing sinister about us so instead of pressing the issue, the single cop on duty took us at our word, sensing our ability to cope and opened some jail cells for us to sleep in. The following morning he even shared his coffee with us and we were again on our way, making it home at last, turning up on the doorstep on the fourth day along with the mailman.

My mother never had a cross word, however. Never even asked how we managed to get back home and within two days had found me another job bailing up musty old paper collected by the Boy Scouts and stored for over a year in a falling down horse stable with a leaky roof. As for my father, how could he see the wrong in that? As I said, he had the equivalent of a second grade education and was forced to stay home and work on his own father's farm almost from the time he could walk. No, not a word from him either. Instead, that was when he bought a lot of paint and had me paint the two story shed out back in my spare time. But, even so, what was there to complain about when it was me and not one of my brothers who got to go along on fishing trips with him and his best friend. And further, when my father went out in the woods to cut down trees for fire wood, I was the one who got to go and even though there was more work involved in helping, my mother always made special sandwiches for the occasion and I also got to drink real coffee that my father heated in a pot over a small campfire.

Another thing that gave my life some importance at the time was playing cards. It was a neighborhood social event that met every month and rotated from house to house in the spring, summer and fall. Twenty people in the group meant five card tables with two couples at each one and the game was called Five Hundred. I always liked to watch and listen to the adult conversations but every so often there would be a person short so I would get to set in. The good part was that no one seemed to regret me as a partner because we still won as many games as anyone else. And then, somewhere in there it was December, 1941 and I can still see the headline on the local paper stating that the Japanese had bombed Pearl Harbor. That was when everything finally began to change for the better financially.

The great depression began in 1929 and finally began to ease in the late thirties but it took the war to bring any major changes to the economy. Soon after it began, the government built a munitions factory about twenty five miles away that made explosives for bombs. My father and several other men from town were able to get good paying jobs there and car pooled back and forth to work where he finally became a supervisor until 1945 when the war ended. It was during that period when my parents were able to make payments and bought the house we lived in. All together I think we lived in that house for nearly eight years and while there are many memories associated with that, only a few still seem to have any significance.

On the dark side a classmate in the third grade fell through the ice on the river and was drowned and left an empty seat in the room where she sat in the row ahead of me. In the fifth grade another girl disappeared and was later found floating in the canal where they thought she fell off the railroad bridge. Another neighbor with kids my age who lived directly across the street from the one who asphyxiated himself, shot and killed himself also.

As for religion, my parents were Methodist and felt it important that we all go to church, plus Sunday School for us kids. It was something I managed to skip later on but not until after I was forced to play the role of Joseph in the annual Christmas play, one of the most embarrassing moments of my life. None of the biblical stories ever made any sense to me either. I could never understand how some guy who lived a long time ago and suffered a lot less than some of the people I knew first hand could be so important. And most disparaging was the idea of having been born sinful. Why would a God who was supposed to have loved us all, done that to us before we were even old enough to have done something wrong? That and the hypocrisy so many people displayed, ended with my refusal to continue going at around fourteen. This upset my mother considerably, leading her to occasionally say that she didn't want any heathens growing up in her house but she never once suggested that I should find another place to live. Ultimately it became another one of those things that no one ever mentioned again.

Then there was the Boy Scouts which my older brother loved. He joined when he was twelve and I was made a member when I became that old and was dragged along for the meetings which seemed to be just another form of silliness to me. Kids wearing uniforms, saluting, taking oaths, working for embroidered patches to sew on their uniforms, thinking it was such a big deal to be able to build a fire and sleep in a tent. I did live through initiation though and spent one week in Boy Scout camp the first summer but that did it for me. In the beginning I skipped as many meetings as possible and my brother was decent enough not to rat on me, but I finally quit altogether. Again, without any repercussions from my parents.

Another enjoyable summer experience between my exiles to my grandfather's farm and the interim jobs my mother kept finding for me was swimming in the lake where we would often spend the whole day. There my companions were usually a kid named Wally and one of his brothers. Wally was my age and it was his older brother who I had shared the Cherry Camp experience with and it was their father who had killed himself with car exhaust. Wally is of note because he was a terrific swimmer and diver and his goal was to someday swim the English Channel. Later, after we had moved away, I learned that he came very close to doing that. Not having much money, he hitch hiked to New York, managed to stow away on the Queen Mary and go to England. Unfortunately, getting off the ship was another matter. With no passport or ticket, he was placed in police custody until his mother was able to send money for a forced trip back home. His dream didn't die there, however, because he moved to California and used to swim offshore in the ocean from Malibu northward for twenty miles to stay in condition for a formal attempt. Sadly enough, just before he had things in order and was ready to go, he was involved in a serious car accident which broke one of his legs, something which never healed properly.

As for myself, at thirteen I began working with my brother at the largest grocery store in town, stocking shelves after school where we were trusted and worked almost without supervision. What was significant about it for me was that, except for canned goods, almost all merchandize was in bulk and no one seemed to care how much we ate for ourselves. And that was where I discovered pears. I loved fresh pears and nearly ate myself sick. The other thing learned from that job was a lesson in psychology and marketing. Take fresh raisins, for example, another product that came in bulk and required weighing and bagging before putting it on display. Two different stakes of bagged raisins on the shelf out front. One would be priced at two pounds for nineteen cents, the one next to it would be priced at two pounds for twenty nine cents. Same raisins out of the same big sack in the back room, different priced but the higher marked ones always seemed to sell as well as the cheaper group.

The next year at fourteen, Wally the swimmer and I both got a job at a gas station where we worked together after school, Saturdays and through one summer. We pumped gas, checked the oil, cleaned windshields, changed oil in cars and greased them. The rule old Jack the owner handed down was as follows. If the owner left his car at the pump with orders to fill it up and check the oil while they went to the bank across the street, we were to charge them for one quart of oil if the car didn't need any and two quarts if if it only needed one. It was something we did if old Jack was around but never if he wasn't. The other thing we did do once in a while though when he wasn't there was to take someone's car for a short joy ride once the vehicle was serviced, too young to be driving, no driver's license if we got caught. Wally, unfortunately, could be a little reckless in other ways too. Once he drove a car off the inside end on the big hoist, put a dent in the bumper and destroyed a barrel of grease. Then he drained the oil from another car, greased it and forgot to put fresh oil in the engine. The owner came, picked it up but never got home before the engine destroyed itself and that was that. Wally got fired and I quit shortly thereafter because my father got a new job in another town and we were moving. The other thing I remember about Wally and his brothers was that they never talked about their deceased father. It just never came up and they went on as if it never happened. Being poor like the rest of us the other thing that sticks out was that he and his brothers would take their old rifle and go up and down the streets shooting squirrels out of the trees which they took home to eat with none of the neighbors ever calling the police or saying a word.

WAUPUN

Thirty three miles east of our old residence, a new town for us. Prison city, location of the state prison for men and the prison for the criminally insane. The first right in the center of town, the other out on the edge. And east of town a few miles, the Horicon Marsh, a huge wetland and one of the largest wildlife refuges in the country. The town itself, about five thousand people at the time, the same as Portage which we left behind. We moved right before school began in the fall. I would be a junior, brother Ted a senior, younger brother George and sister Ida both ninth graders and my father was the mechanic for the new Jeep dealership in town. Not much of any significance happened that first year. Made a few friends, worked in the garage after school, learned to play tennis and had my first girlfriend. She lived about a block away and we usually walked to school together and did our homework at the kitchen table at her house while her parents sat out in the living room which didn't keep us from doing a little quiet necking once in a while. We also skipped school a couple of times and hitch hiked over to Fondu lac, a much larger town, just for the fun of it. Senior year was different, however. I had spent most of the summer either working for my father or working at the canning factory and went out for football in the fall, something my father felt unimportant. I should be working instead. And that brings up the subject of Eddie Luck.

Football practice began a month before school started so there I was out on the field in the B team, playing left guard during scrimmage. The opposing right guard on the A team was Eddy. Eddy liked to play rough and dirty. He was down there facing me with fist already doubled up and every time the ball was snapped he came across the line deliberately aiming for the gut. Two or three times was enough of that, however. It wasn't one of those things one thinks out clearly. Instinct just seemed to come into play instead.

Face to face, the ball was in play and Eddy came roaring across the line but that time I backed up half a step which got him off balance just enough for me to dump him over on his back and then charge down the field to see if I could make the tackle. No tackle but once the play was over and everyone turned around, there was Eddy, flat on his back, and he was not moving. Not even realizing what I had done at first, it soon became clear that I had ran over him, end to end, with cleated football shoes on. Besides stepping on his leg and his stomach, I thought I had also put his eye out because it was a pool of blood. Fortunately or not, it only looked that way because a cleat had caught him on the forehead just above the eye instead. Needless to say Eddy was far less oppositional during practice after that and the other players seemed to look at me a little differently. Then school started and before football season was over, shocked and embarrassed by it, my girlfriend and I were voted Homecoming Queen and King. We went together through the winter but broke up that spring.

As an aside to that, it was somewhere in there that I learned that Eddy was parentless. Raised by an uncle, he had no idea who his mother or father were. We also ended up in the same English class together.

The teacher was young, not too long out of college, and there was Eddy, determined to go his own way. In an attempt to improve his behavior, she put him in the front row, right in front of her desk. The first day he behaved himself reasonably well. The second day he brought a paper back novel with him and the minute she turned away to write on the blackboard he pulled his desk chair up close, put his feet up on her desk, took out his book and started to read. She told him to stop and pulled his chair back. He ignored her. She said it again. He still ignored her. The she left the room and came back with the principal.

The principal ordered him to get up and leave the room. Eddy refused to obey. The principal went across the hall, got the biology teacher and the two men dragged Eddy, desk and all, out of the room. One weeks suspension and Eddy was back with only a slight change in attitude. He didn't stop smoking in the halls, either, and before year end had probably accumulated a dozen or more days of suspension.

And then there was Eddy's cousin, Rosy, also in our class. Eddy didn't have a father and neither did Rosy. She hardly had a mother, either. And if she did, I never met her. She was always gone at night, hanging out in a bar somewhere so Rosy's house was where all the parties were. Not doing anything? Get some beer, drive by Rosy's. If she was home, go on in. Soon the place would be full of under age drinkers having a good time. As opposed to Eddy, Rosie was very straight. She liked to neck a little but that was it. No one made out with Rosie. Not so for Eddy and a classmate named Patty. Rosie's house was quite small. The main bedroom was right off the living room and one night Eddy and Patty were having sex in the bedroom with the door open. Well, think what you may about Patty, but just a few weeks later she was killed in an auto crash, and so much for moralizing. Those are the things that help change one's perspective.

As for Eddy, he did graduate, but never having exactly been friends, we went our separate ways. I did hear that he beat up a security guard at a dance hall and then, riding around with his buddies one night, he saw a hitch hiker and had them stop. He got out, slammed the poor man right in the face with his fist and proceeded to beat him up without anyone trying to stop it. Next I heard he enlisted in the Air Force and I didn't see him until our twentieth class reunion and there he was, still looking for a confrontation, trying to provoke a fight. He had retired after twenty years in the service and came back to that dumpy, dismal little town, only to become the town drunk and proceeded to drink himself to death before he reached fifty five.

Rosie, meanwhile, continued to have parties at her house for the summer after graduation, we were still friends and many was the summer night when I walked home after the sun was up. Then some farm kid fell in love with her and thought she was destined to be his girl friend, even though they had never had a real date together. As a result, he caught me walking her home early one evening and drove his pickup clear across the lawn of the church on the corner and seriously tried to run me down. Then, minutes later, he showed up at her house with a small caliber revolver in hand, convinced he had to shoot me. Rosie talked to him. I talked to him. Eventually he calmed down a little and then I expressed an interest in his weapon. What kind was it, where did he get it and a lot of other dumb questions and damned if he didn't just hand it to me. Crisis defused, I looked it over, took the bullets out of it and gave it back to him. He apologized, Rosie gave him a clear idea of what she didn't want to happen between them and he drove off.

When it came to the rest of my senior year in High School, I can't say I was an exceptional student. But I did remember some of my teachers as compared to school back in Portage where I remember none of them. I worked very hard in geometry class because I thought the teacher was gorgeous. The science teacher, however, took me aside and told me he knew I could do a lot better than I was doing if I'd stop goofing off with some of the others in his class. But as for the English teacher, her treatment was special. I always did all the homework, paid attention in class and got good grades. I was a bit puzzled though, when she gave in class writing assignments. The first time we began and everyone was working, she came back to my desk and quietly told me that I didn't have to do it. If I wanted I could go to the library instead, no explanation given. After that, when she would occasionally repeat the assignment, she would look at me and just nod an approval, where upon I got up quietly and left the room. I could only speculate as to the reason behind it but it did seem very special and it was the one class I actually got an A in. And then I graduated. I was seventeen. That left me in a huge state of panic. I couldn't afford to go to college and my parents certainly couldn't afford to send me. My father in fact, thought that would be waste of time. I needed to get a job instead, something my mother somewhat seconded, having said far too many times that she just wanted her kids to grow up and amount to something. Whatever that was supposed to mean specifically, I still haven't figured out, even after all these years.

A small town of about five thousand people, there were no job fairs, no recruiters came to town, no internet to do searches on, no large industry. The choices came down to just two. Work in the rivet factory or a small factory that made metal cans to put evaporated milk in. I ended up loading metal cans into boxcars. The boss was a weasily little man who always stood by the time clock in the morning and if you were even one minute late, you lost half an hour's pay, so where was I supposed to go from there? I didn't have the faintest idea and the only good thing about it was that I had earned enough money to buy an used car. A 1929, old box of a thing, Chevy which in a deal that made absolutely no sense to me, some guy wanted to trade his 1935 Chrysler for, even up. It was a big eight cylinder, ahead of it's time style wise monster with overdrive which was great fun to drive and something I rolled over going eighty shortly after I got it. A very solid car, the only damage was some dents in the roof and running boards bent up so far the doors wouldn't open. A relatively easy fix. Later I bought a welder, learned how to weld and converted the vehicle from a four door into a coupe with a sun roof and drove the thing for three more years. As for my, what was I going to do with my life dilemma, once again my mother did her thing.

STRINGING WIRE

A quart of beer with twenty shots of whiskey in it may not be a big deal to some people but if you're seventeen and the twenty guys who put the whiskey in the beer are all older, bigger and a hell of a lot tougher than you are, you had better make a serious attempt to drink some of it. I drank. It was my official introduction to a new way of life and to a peculiar kind of comradeship that would be shared on and off for the next three years.

My mother managed to get me the job through the help of an old family friend and former neighbor back in Portage named George. A very admirable guy, once. Or so it seemed when I was a kid. He was the one who went fishing on the river with my father. He also loved to hunt and tell stories and helped my father with a variety of projects that ranged from building boats to transplanting Chevy parts into Fords to keep them running during the war years when they stopped making new automobiles. Back then he worked for the power company as the local representative and service man. But that was six years earlier, the last time I had seen him.

This time I tracked him down in a small town bar in northern Wisconsin where he was drinking with Ralph, his boss, now our boss, the crew leader. I was there the night before so I could start work in the morning. It was a Wednesday evening and I remember it clearly. George looked absolutely horrible. Thin, worn and emaciated at forty five. Nothing but a dim copy of the former robust and hearty individual I remembered. He was instead the victim of too much alcohol and too much hard living. Completely shocked, I left them after one beer and checked into the local hotel and went to bed early, not at all sure how the following day would turn out.

Hung over, George seemed morose and preoccupied in the morning and was back in the bar again after work. The next day was a repeat. And what did I know? It was none of my business so I worked hard and kept my mouth shut and wondered how working together would turn out in the long run. Basically, we were the inspection crew. Ralph and George climbed poles and steel towers checking the leakage of high voltage insulators along power lines. My job was to the carry the long handled instrument and hand it up to them once they had climbed part way up and then to record the pole or tower number in a notebook along with the readings. Then in those situations where the power line didn't run along a road and went cross country instead, it was my job to walk back to the truck when we were half way through and drive it around to the next cross road and walk back in. George was in the senior position, I was the flunky, but still. It must have been hard for him to have me see him like that. Something I tried hard to pretend I didn't notice.

We worked together for those two long days before going home for the weekend and it was good to be there while it lasted. I had been out all Saturday night with

126

Joyce. We had parked out in the woods in the county park where we had spent the night talking and necking in the back seat of my car until the sun broke though the trees in the morning. Then we started riding around town, trying to waste enough time so that it would be a reasonable hour for her to be coming home from her girlfriend's house where she was supposed to have spent the night.

That strategy went well enough until I turned off Main onto a cross street and spotted my parent's car coming toward us. They flagged us down and pulled up along side.

My father had been on my case before about some of the late hours and the beer drinking because I was still a minor so I rolled down the window and waited for it to begin. One look at their faces, however, told me that wasn't it at all. Instead, they could hardly speak. George, the old family friend from the past and the man I now worked with, had died the day before and they were on the way to his house to be with his wife. His death was ruled accidental. A kindness, I believe. Somehow a man who has been around guns all his life just doesn't get the wrong end of a loaded shotgun pointed at himself so it blows the top of his head off. Suicide wasn't something new, however. George was now the third man from the old neighborhood to have made that choice. As discussed earlier, the first left his car motor running in the closed garage one evening. The other man had been exposed to mustard gas in the war and his lungs were half eaten away, causing him to get sick a lot and cough up blood. He shot himself, too. But neither of them were old friends like George and it was a difficult time for my parents. As for myself, I will never know for sure. Did it have anything to do with me? What if I had never taken the job? Was I some reminder out of the past of better times and better things that suddenly became too difficult to deal with? How could I ever be sure? Later, however, back at work I learned that George's life had been heavily complicated by an unhappy marriage, another woman and alcoholism. But still....

As for Ralph the boss, while being one of the easiest men to work for I ever met, he too, was an alcoholic. How he managed, I will never know but what had to be done, got done. Some days I wondered why he never lost his grip and fell off a pole or a tower or died of alcohol poisoning or just disappeared from heaving his guts out but he didn't and by the end of our first year together we had personally ridden and walked from one end of the state to the other in about fifteen different directions and drank a beer or two in over half the bars in the territory. Then I was transferred to one of the much larger work crews. That was when I did my best to down that huge glass of beer with the fifteen shots of whiskey in it. Those fifteen shots came from the crew. My new boss did not add to it though. He rarely drank. An occasional single beer with the men once in a while but that was it. A devoted but extremely tolerant family man, he knew his people's strengths and limitations, had their respect and used them efficiently.

There were two other non drinkers in the bunch, Baldy and Shuck as they were called. One married, one not, but left alone and how they spent their evenings I never knew. The rest, however, all spent varying amounts of their after work hours in a bar. Back then hotels didn't have television sets or libraries. For those who wanted more out of life, the bar room was it. Even though I was under legal age I tagged along, playing the role of manhood, listened to their stories and tried not to keep up with their drinking. The stories were the best part and if you could get them talking soon enough it kept them from

128

making a contest out of drinking in which case some of them became considerably less social than they might otherwise be.

For a bunch of guys whose favorite expression was, talk is cheap, it takes money to buy whiskey, they did an awful lot of taking once they got started. In those few short years I had know them they had rebuilt every power line they had ever worked on dozens of times and had relived a multitude of other fascination adventures along the way. It was a tough and dangerous job even in the best of weather and there were some casualties. The suicide, an electrocution, a friend dead from a fall high off a pole. It was part of the job, a part that got tougher when the weather became harsh because of the awful things it could do to power lines, equipment and people. It was still a heavily power dependent society even back in those days and if something broke, fell down or burned up, it had to be fixed as soon as possible, even if it meant working around the clock in the freezing winter rain.

When the rain fell, it froze on the power line wires. When it did the ice built up to the point where the wire couldn't carry the extra weight and down it came, helped along by the wind whipping it back and forth. And because of some of the extreme high voltages involved, it was a serious danger to man and beast, sometimes even creating fires in spite of the wet and cold. As for repairing the damage and restoring power to the companies customers, that was our responsibility. If it started raining on a Friday evening and you had just spent the day hanging off the side of a hundred foot tower in the northern part of the state fighting the cold, you got in one of the trucks along with the rest of the crews and headed south over ice coated roads under conditions that could turn a four or five hour drive into eight or nine hours. If you could keep a big enough hole scrapped through the frost on the inside of the windshield and if the sound of the tire chains slapping against the wheel wells of the truck didn't make you crazy, you put on a few more layers of clothing and went to work when you arrived, even if it was two in the morning. And, if it was still raining, which it probably was, clothing would immediately become board stiff as the wind blew the freezing water through the fabric, clear to the bone, making everything nearly impossible including seeing, walking and staying alive.

It was even more difficult to climb a pole with a heavy tool belt on, buckle off and get something done as the pole and the wires swayed in the wind. Then, by the time a span between two poles was repaired and up, the one behind might well have fallen back down, and as long as the rain kept falling it was one of those situations that kept repeating itself. When you got so tired and cold you couldn't work anymore you crawled in the back of the truck and tried to sleep, huddled in the corner along with a few other frozen souls. Sometimes it would rain for two days straight and once it stopped it still took a day or two to finish so it was a long time between hotel rooms and showers. No wonder these guys drank, told stories and made up offbeat expressions. Some of them did other things too. Like pay for sex. Not much to brag about but a few of them viewed it as an accomplishment never-the-less.

Married or single, it made no difference. After a few drinks off they went. But hookers didn't stand around on street corners waiting to be picked up back then. They didn't have to. They worked in a house of ill-repute or in the back room of some bar or down some country road in a farm house and in many towns and counties it was completely legal. Or at least overlooked.

As for myself, there were a lot of good reasons why a sensible person wouldn't want to do that, single or married but when the opportunity presented itself, they would still opt for it. Of course there was always pressure to drag someone else into this debauchery but fortunately I was never one to just be one of the boys. But again, what did I know? Perhaps I wasn't old enough or hadn't been out in the weather long enough to appreciate such things.

These were also the days before paid vacations, sick leave and personal business time off. The only recognized holidays were Thanksgiving, Christmas, New Years and the Fourth of July, and then only if nothing fell down, broke or shorted out. If that didn't happen the only other days we got to stay indoors was if the temperature dropped below zero. That was the criteria. They hadn't invented the wind chill factor yet either so it didn't matter if the job involved having to hang off the side of a cold steel tower on the edge of Lake Michigan in a forty mile per hour wind. If it was above zero, you went to work.

One winter it dropped to fifty three below zero in the northern part of the state. It was so cold the power line wires shrank so much they pulled up against the cross arms of the poles and burned in two. Of course we weren't anywhere near there when that happened, either. That seemed to be the unwritten rule. No matter what part of the territory you were you were always at least half a state away from where the trouble was. Not that it made any difference but it was only thirty five below where we were when we got the call. It was so cold that none of the half dozen trucks would start so we built a fire under the crankcase of one of the biggest to warm the oil to the point where it would turn over. Once started, we used it to pull the rest of them and get them running. Except for the jeep. It was so stiff all four wheels just skidded over the frozen ground without turning. We left it behind.

This was also the time before thermal underwear, down parkas and a lot of other good things so there we were, out there with so many layers of clothes on one couldn't bend over, scratch their butt or touch their nose, the snow squeaking from the cold and the fierce, icy wind doing its awesome, nasty number on everything in sight. To say the least, it was a grueling existence and that was a part of it, the weather. The other part was the brutally hard work.

Power lines always took the shortest distance between two points and it didn't matter what was in the way, whether it was miles of swamp, trees, brush and boulders or cow pasture. If we couldn't get the trucks in, we tried the jeep. If we couldn't get the jeep in we hand pulled a winch line across the expanse and dragged in what we needed. If that didn't work, we walked, carrying ropes, tools and two hundred pound rolls of wire on our backs, hand dug and manually lifted poles into their new holes with ropes and prys. In the process we used up a lot of shovels and breaker bars on rocks which always seemed to be halfway down any hole that needed to be at least three feet deeper. Occasionally, dynamite helped.

Spring and fall could be beautiful, however, and some of the summers were very special because it was gratifying to be outside all day in the warm weather. I was strong and healthy and it felt good to flex my muscles and exercise my growing knowledge of the world. I loved new towns and new people and a growing association with the odd assortment of characters I had to work with. That part didn't come easy, though, and I went through a period of jockeying for position with the younger guys, all still older than me. Maybe more than usual because I wouldn't accept a secondary role in their social structure. Ultimately, it was finally resolved in a snow bank one cold night outside the hotel after work. There was a big farm kid six years older than I, four inches taller and at least twenty pounds heavier. His name was Vince and for some reason he didn't like something I said and invited me outside.

The only advantage I enjoyed over this guy was that I was quicker and a hell of a lot smarter but he still did me a lot of damage before I got him pinned down on his back. Then I had to beat both my fist and his face to a pulp before he was willing to quit. In the process I had to get his thumb in my mouth and draw blood to keep him from scratching my eyes out. When we first retreated back into the bar I looked like the loser with blood seeping from the gouges on my face where he had scratched me but that changed an hour later. By then I had stopped bleeding but his face had gotten blacker and blacker as his lips and eyes swelled up to the point where he couldn't talk and could hardly see. I was was well healed withing a week but he was still carrying around some big puffy spots tinted with black and blue. Needless to say I was allowed to walk in my own space after that.

Once spring came that year, however, we finally got down to working only five or six days a week and on free weekends I would come home to see Joyce who was still my friend. We stopped trying to make out, however, because even though she wanted to, it still frightened her so we settled down to raiding her father's liquor cabinet and discussing Phillip Wylie books. Then summer came. Joyce turned seventeen and she and her girlfriend stole her friend's father's car and ran away from home. Three months later they found the car and her friend in Montana. But no Joyce. I missed her terribly the first several months but always knew that wherever she was, she was still alive. Eventually I met a girl my age named Margie and went with her until one day, about a year after she had left, Joyce called home from Alabama. Thanks to her father, she was back within a couple of days and that is when she called me. There wasn't much she wanted to share except for the fact that she had gotten married in the meantime, something her father immediately had annulled because she was still under age. Other than that when I brought her home after our first night out she she made it very clear she was no longer a virgin and would be legally an adult in a few more days.

In our changed relationship, her father also contributed to the fun. In his mind I was the only good influence in her life. As a result he would sometimes give me a few big bills and the keys to his car so I could take Joyce to dinner or a movie, something we actually did on a few occasions. Other times we would spend the evening in the back seat of his car instead and use the money to play poker with later on in a back room down at the bowling alley.

Unfortunately for me during that period I had to spend three weekends in a row out of town working. But then, by the time I got back, Joyce had met an older married man and wouldn't go out with me anymore. That affair lasted until she ran away again. I heard she was in Chicago and then St. Louis. Finally she was back in town for Christmas. I didn't call her and she didn't call me but I saw her at her house when I went to a party that her older sister had invited me to. I came into the living room and there she was, just sitting there smiling at me like nothing at all had happened.

She had been my friend and my girlfriend both, a source of joy and anguish who had helped me stay anchored in the real world away from work and then abandoned me in the end. Pretty as ever, I looked at her and was suddenly angry. Then, before I realized what I was doing I walked up to her and poured a full bottle of beer all over her hair and clothes. About that time her father came in the front door, saw what I had done and threw me off the front porch. I only saw her once after that. It was about two years later when she was in the hospital. Married again, she had had a baby and was hemorrhaging badly. I don't know where her husband was but she had asked a friend to come and find me, instead. We talked a little, mostly about nothing and I left, never to return or follow up on what happened to her.

During the course of the three years I worked at this job, I quit twice. Once in the winter when I drove my old car down to Florida and spent two weeks with some people who had come up to the lake in the summer. I quit again when my older brother, a Marine stationed in California, was shipped out to Korean when that war started. My parents went to bring his car and his other personal possessions home and I decided to go along. It was supposed to be a thirty nine hour ride on the train from Chicago to Los Angeles but took two and a half days because of flooded tracks and an engine failure. After finally picking up the car at the Marine Base and a brief visit with a relative, we headed home.

It was the middle of July. Las Vegas was a very small town at the time, alone out in the middle of an immense desert. The Golden Nugget was the largest casino there, sitting at the downtown crossroads of two lane streets. We didn't stop. North of Vegas about twenty miles we were climbing a long, steep hill in the midday heat when the car's engine began clanking. My father nursed the car along until we came to a gas station and motel where we had to wait to get the car repaired. The thermometer on the side of the station said it was over a hundred and twenty.

Two days later we were on the road again and things went smoothly until Cheyenne, Wyoming. There the timing chain on the engine broke. I left my parents behind at that point, found the bus terminal and took the

Greyhound back home. I ended up sitting next to a cute girl from Iowa who said I should come and see her sometime. I did. Twice on weekends, later, after I called my boss and got my old job back. She lived in a small town along the Mississippi, population a hundred at most. We carved pumpkins together at Halloween and went to a down home square dance in the church but, all in all, she just lived too far away.

Five months after I turned twenty one I got a letter in the mail telling me to report for a physical. I was being inducted into the military. Why? Because I wasn't going to college like some of my former high school classmates were able to do. Very discriminatory, I felt and it made me very angry. If it hadn't been for my mother I might well have sought asylum in Canada and felt justified in doing so. Fortunately I did not and only later would I be able to see that such idealism would have been a serious mistake. That was because getting drafted turned out to be a blessing in disguise, the thing that rescued me from spending the rest of my life working for the power company, which I was often concerned about. But how to solve that problem, I didn't have any idea at the time. Small town mentality, no higher education, no mentor, no nothing except hard work and not enough money. No clear way to break free. Not that working for the power company was all bad.

Most certainly I was older and wiser because of it and had shared some unique experiences with the men I worked with. In the end, however, none of them turned out to be close friends and only two of them were in any way special. One was Bob, about ten years older than I. Married and faithful. But he, too, liked to drink a bit. One time after several hours in the bar room we went out to dinner. Bob ordered a steak but it slipped off his plate when he tried to cut it so he pushed his plate aside and sliced it up right on the table top. Then he took out the short stub of a cigar he had puffed on earlier and tried to re light it. Unfortunately, because the cigar was so short, he ended by burning all the skin off the end of his nose instead.

Then one day he took a corner in the company truck too fast and rolled it over. Luckily he was unhurt but our boss wasn't too happy. The other thing about him was that he really wasn't comfortable climbing poles. Sadly, one day they were working live wires and he missed a step before he got buckled off, brushed a twelve hundred volt line and fell off the pole onto his back. The only good thing about it for me was that I wasn't there to see him die.

The other individual I liked was Dutch. An ex navy man, he had been a deep sea diver. Before he was discharged he managed to appropriate a full deep sea diving suit along with hoses and air pump which he kept on his boat, a large old wooden hulled craft named the Should-have-sunk which was moored out on the big lake near his home. He continued to dive for fun, for salvage and for a body when someone disappeared in the lake. Dutch was climbing poles and towers when I left and it was only later that I learned that he had gotten tangled up in the one hundred and thirty eight thousand volt line.

As for my mandatory service to my country, there I was one day, on the train, headed south for boot camp. I was to become a ground pounder, slang for the U.S. Army. Although my request at induction was to be in an intelligence unit, I was sent to the Signal Corps instead. Camp Gordon Georgia, not far from Atlanta. Still far better than the Infantry, although that didn't prevent some of the men I was with from being sent to Korea after basic training where they got themselves killed. And what a training to go into battle with. Six weeks.

Our basic weapon was a 30 Carbine, essentially useless except in close combat. We marched a lot, did a lot of push ups, did KP, got to shoot fifteen rounds of ammo with our rifles, threw one hand grenade, went on a five mile and an eight mile hike and crawled on our bellies through the mud under a barbed wire enclosure while someone shot live machine gun rounds over our heads. After that, a short furlough and I was made an instructor on the base instead of getting sent overseas. That kept me in the states for another eight months. Then a two week furlough on which I was able to see my grandfather for the last time. It was February and he was in the cold back bedroom of a small shack of a house where he and my grandmother ended up, hardly able to talk and soon dead. Then my orders were to report to San Francisco to get on a ship and go to Okinawa.

Fifteen miles wide and sixty miles long, Okinawa was sub tropical and had been in U.S. hands since WWII. The invasion had cost the lives of thirty thousand American troops along with a far larger number of Japanese but by the time I arrived in 1951 it had two Air Force bases on it. One was for long range B29 bombers, the other for fighter jets. The Korean war was now in process and most of the bombing was done from this small island. Not our mission, however. I was with a small army company attached to the air force and it was our job to install and maintain telephone communications. That sometimes meant being down in a ditch with a jack hammer trying to cut through coral rock.

I spent the first few months at the bomber base where the main company was located but soon got transferred to the fighter base on the south end of the island where we were just a small group of about twenty with only a Sargent in charge. This meant no dress rehearsals, inspections or reviews and a couple of vehicles to ride around the island in on weekends. Unfortunately, six months later I was transferred back to company headquarters, something I thought I would regret. That was until about a week later when the new company commander, A Captain, called me in and offered me a job in the headquarters's office.

He did this because he had gone through all the records and found that in the battery of tests we had to take when inducted, I had the highest test scores of anyone in the company, several college grads included. To him that meant I should be doing something besides splicing telephone wires back together. I thanked him for the offer, didn't like the idea of sitting in an office all day and told him I didn't know how to type. He thought about that for a moment and came up with a different idea.

Every Saturday when us troops all fell out for review, he would always give a very short speech about some timely topic of interest so how would I like to be his speech writer? It sounded good to me. My only responsibility. Go to the library, do a little research and that was it. The rest of the time I was on my own. I could do anything I wanted, on or off the base and that was how I spent the last six months of my tour of duty. This meant that for one thing, I had a lot of time to read and actually read over a hundred books. It was a situation that reminded me of my high school English teacher who allowed me to leave class and not have to do the writing assignments others had to complete. It also gave me a lot of time to write letters which led to something else after my discharge.

Most of my letters went to my first cousin Alicia who was a year younger than I and lived in Cleveland, Ohio. Originally, she had lived back in Portage just three blocks away and walked the path that cut through the vacant lot adjacent to my family's house on the way to school. So long ago now, but so clearly still, the image of her smiling, and the allure. If only I had had the courage at the time and some idea as to how, I would have loved to have held hands and maybe even kissed her, but I never did. Not back then anyway. But we did manage to hang out together at picnics and other family gatherings during those early years and in spite of daydreams, that was that.

Then, when I was ten, her father was killed in an auto accident and soon thereafter her mother moved away in an attempt to leave the pain behind. Five hundred miles away so it was always a year or two between the times when we got to see each other again, and then only for a few hours here and there while they came to visit family and friends until her mother finally remarried. That ended the visits until I was out of school, working and old enough to have my own car and so, adoring her still, I drove that five hundred miles myself. What I hadn't considered however, was that since I was old enough to be on my own, so was she and by now she was actually living with some older man across town from her mother.

But we got to see each other, never-the-less, that long afternoon when her, whatever he was, was at work and puppy love and teen aged yearning finally found their way through the confusion without consideration of future promise or complication and gave life a bolder perspective for sure. And now, writing to her, I, a man and she, a woman from the past, who suddenly seemed far more significant to me than anything else life had presented me with that far. So much so that the months of correspondence finally led to the moment where, back in the States for discharge from the military, I took the train to Cleveland where she lived, bought a used car and picked her up. Together we drove to the military base in Kentucky I was to be discharged from, took out a marriage license that wasn't completely factual, found a small town preacher and became a couple.

Surprised as my parents had to have been, they accepted her openly nonetheless, as her mother did me. It wasn't that. Much of it was other relatives, self righteous as they were, along with others who needed to voice an opinion. But larger than that and more intrusive were some of the events of the past. Things largely beyond her control but devastating still which, coupled with the uniqueness of our relationship, were hard to overcome. We talked of moving to California and perhaps should have but at the time it just seemed too far away. We did get to spend the summer living together, however, and well into the fall without regret. But then, on a different level, we both seemed to know how it had to end. Not because we didn't care, but more so that we did. We had a four day long, special reunion several months later which was our way of finally saying goodbye. No regrets, either. Not a one. We had crossed a few lines but got to live out a part of our fantasy in the process and how can anyone be condemned for that, our personal declaration of independence in defying convention?

COLLEGE

Much as I resented the discriminatory nature of the draft laws and the forced life style of the military, in all honesty, it was one of the better things that had happened to me thus far. Not for the actual experiences but for the opportunity that came with it. College was now possible because of the GI Bill and I was able to enroll at the University of Wisconsin in the spring semester after my cousin and I parted. I was not a promising prospect according to my frumpily dressed counselor, however. After looking at where I had graduated in my high school class and considering the fact that I hadn't been in a class room for seven years, she gave me a hard look, told me I was wasting my time and stated that I wouldn't even make it through the first semester, seeming to have overlooked what got me accepted in the first place. Once again it was test scores. I topped out somewhere in the upper five percent in the entrance exams. I couldn't defend myself and remind her of that, however, because I didn't even know it until later. So, what did I say instead? Nothing.

I walked out of her office and never went back. Not even after getting all solid Bs that first semester and making honors before graduating. I never went to my graduation ceremony either. Should have, maybe, because it was a struggle to have gotten that far. Married by then, two children, working nights for two years, summers full time and odd jobs for the rest but when it was done I was able to sit behind a desk in a temperature controlled environment with lots of fringe benefits for the rest of my working life. But that doesn't mean that I never thought about those other days, back when I was younger. Summer heat, pounding rain, snow banks and blizzards, ice and wind. Life and death and other challenges too. But first, in the fall before starting college, another story, the most important one of all.

The TV blared and the low ceilinged living room was full of cigarette smoke. Father, mother, two brothers, a sister, and no introductions, I was left to wait and be looked over. A huge ashtray on a stand by the couch had at least two hundred old cigarette butts in it as her father puffed away while the mother stood in the kitchen door and looked at me. And so much for blind dates, I thought, as I sat there feeling uncomfortable. Where was she? And why wasn't she ready? It was a little too late to back out now, however. As for my sister, the instigator who arranged it, I could only thank her later.

Actually the wait probably wasn't really that long because the stairway door soon opened and my date stepped into the room, ready to go. Except for her mother, there were no goodbyes, no, have a nice time, good wishes from any of the family and all I could do was to follow this young woman out to the car where I still had enough good sense to open the door for her.

It was a graduation party for the nursing school where my sister and she had spent the last three years sharing a room in the dormitory together. First in their class, it seemed impossible that my date could have been a member of the family I had just met. Maybe she hadn't noticed but I felt I mumbled and stumbled over words a lot that evening, rather awed by the person I was able to hold when we danced. Attractive, yes. Very. Beyond that there were few, if any, appropriate words. Precious might have been a part of it because when we danced I was afraid to hold her too tight. I didn't want to crush her, I just wanted to look into her eyes, watch her smile and listen to her voice. After that we dated and kept on dating through the winter and into spring where I was then going to the university where the main part of the campus abutted a beautiful, deep water lake. That next summer my blind date, now working as an emergency room nurse, and I each came up with enough money to purchase a vintage old Chris Craft runabout which we kept tied to a buoy on the lake. It was something to go for a spin on in the evening and use for water skiing on weekends. One of the best times of our lives. My, one day to be wife, all slim and sexy in her two piece bathing suit smiling up at me, the old boat skimming over the water, the wind in our hair, it was a memorable time indeed.

Eventually, of course, some good things have to end. Graduation approached and the old boat was sold so we could move on. Married now and with children, we first went to Ohio for nine months and then on to California. There our new house was on a gracefully curved, palm lined street back before all the orange groves and strawberry fields had been torn up and paved over. In the front yard, setting the tone, a huge Jacaranda tree carpeted the lawn in the spring with a layer of blue flowers as bright azaleas and pastel camellias added to the color while, hidden somewhere, a night blooming jasmine wafted through our bedroom window after dark.

And in the back there were banana palms, bougainvillea, honeysuckle and hydrangea along with pampas grass, philodendrons, pyrocantha, poinsettia and out of sight deep amongst the shrubs, a playhouse full of children's toys and laughter. A most beautiful place, it was the house my wife wanted to live in, at least until all our children were through high school. Something I agreed with entirely. And what could be better than in the evening, after the day was done, seeing three little children cuddled close around their mother as she read them bedtime stories before tucking them in with hugs and kisses.

Far more so than boating on the lake ever could have been, living there was the most significant part of our lives. But the lake was still important because it had brought us to the point where we eloped and got married. So was a trip to Yellowstone where we spent an adventurous honeymoon. Then, just a few short years later, sometime unexpected.

Somehow on that, just another warm and sunny, southern California day my eight year old daughter found her way through the maze of corporate phones to my desk.

"What's wrong?" I asked when I heard her voice, she, the oldest of three.

"Mommy fell down and she can't get up," was her reply.

It was a long, long eight miles to home, and dangerous, running two red lights and a stop sign in such a hurry to get there as soon as possible.

Just a few months, a few short months later in early February, and she was gone. I was there in the hospital by her side, a little after four in the morning. So quiet at that time of night. No one, not another soul nearby except for the single nurse on duty. Months of surgery and chemotherapy had taken their toll. She was only thirty two, I was thirty six.

Decades have passed now, and yet, still echoing down through all the long labyrinths of life's twisting corridors my child's voice still lingers, and haunts, as does the memory of other times and places. Her mother's voice, too. Her mother's warmth and beauty, her bright blue eyes. Walks along the river bank, nights with moonlight through the trees, so soon gone.

Long ago now, I only made one trip back to that beautiful lake but I remember it clearly. It was another of those days, languid and serene and perfect except that I was alone this time, standing there on the shore. But the breeze was at my back and had come up strong enough to carry the handful of ashes I had tossed into the air out across that expanse of water where they settled onto the surface of that deep and wondrous place. So too, at Yellowstone. Wind and ashes. More ashes in the wind. And in the yard back in California where they dusted the flowers as I tried to say goodbye. What I didn't know at the time, however, is that it would become something impossibly unable to do with any finality, no matter how many years went by.

After the funeral my parents stayed until my mother thought she had found the ideal live-in housekeeper for me. She was twenty one, from a European country and came highly recommended by the woman she had just worked for. Everything went well for about a month. The children seemed to like her, she was able to clean house and cook. Then one day when she was out somewhere, I took a peak into her room. Everything looked fine except that the bed wasn't made and what was that sticking out from under the sheets? Nothing except some of the bath towels that seemed to be missing, and, good grief, this woman was still wetting the bed at her age and it was a mess.

The next one was a little older and also did a good job. With no car of her own, I would often give her a ride here or there. But then, instead of me telling her which nights she could have off, she started telling me. Not such a serious matter at first, but irritating. Then I happened to look under the wet bar in the house and notice that a couple of my liquor bottles were nearly empty and since I never drank alone and had had no visitors, I put some marks on the labels of the rest and rechecked a little later. This girl was drinking a lot.

Number three housekeeper was purposely a lot older. Middle aged and honest enough to tell me why she needed a place to stay. She had been in a serious car accident and someone had been killed. She had also lost her job, had no family in the area and very little money but she was a great substitute mother and stayed with us for nearly six months, never a problem between us. She also understood my situation and my need to leave the house once the kids were in bed and never once asked for a night out of her own. As for the kids, the early evenings and weekends were our thing. Walk over to the mall for ice cream cones, go to the park and play on the swings, go to their favorite restaurant for dinner, read some books or play games. Then off I would go, night after night in search of something impossible to find. A face in the crowd, on the beach, in the mall, maybe a night club somewhere, lots of nightclubs, lots of faces, none of them the right one, thirty six thousand miles on a new car in a six months period and still needing to go to work the next day. Much as I wished she could have stayed, this live-in housekeeper finally left to go back east and live with a sister. .

Unable to find a ready replacement, I was forced to hire the young girl next door as a baby sitter. Be there when the kids got out of school and sometimes in the evening, something which she could only do two nights a week. Forced as it was, the change of pace was good. More rest, I began facing the reality of my situation a little more openly. Then I was able to find another full time house keeper. She was also middle aged and had her own up-front story to tell. She occasionally liked to drink a beer before going to bed.

Seeing no problem with that, I agreed it was okay as long as she kept it at a minimum and things were fine for several months. She was also exceptionally good with the kids and even went so far as to bake cookies that had little notes inside like fortune cookies and everything was great for several months. The kids were happy, I stopped chasing other women and started going with a secretary from work. But then the housekeeper went to stay with her sister for a weekend, got into a terrible fight with her, stopped on the way home, did some heavy drinking and came back fairly drunk. Still angry and grumbling about her sister, I gave her an ultimatum. Shut up and go to bed, or leave.

Well, poor woman, I guess I felt sorry for her because I gave her a reprieve and all was fine again. For quite a while, at least. Then she went to see her sister again and came home drunk as before, cussing and ranting and refused to calm down. Now one in the morning, I called her son. He said he guessed I would have to call the police because he was too tired to come over.

The next housekeeper was a little younger and I was now in the habit of looking in their room once in a while and about a month later, there was a piece of my wife's jewelry laying on her dresser, so that ended that. There were also a couple more babysitters along the way but by then (which was now about a year and a half after my wife died) I was in an exclusive relationship with a secretary from work.

A few months after that I got an attractive job offer from a major company in Minneapolis which also included moving expenses. As stated in an earlier chapter, this woman, Jolene, had a child who needed a father and I had three children who needed a mother. And although several years younger than I, she had a lot going for her. Attractive, very intelligent, a great cook, knew how to sew on buttons and make beautiful clothes, cleaned house, great with money, handled people well and a lot more. I was older, well employed and a decent human being. A matter of mutual convenience, why ask for anything more?

Therefore, considering the job offer which was an opportunity to leave my house and lots of old memories behind, she suggested and planned our wedding while I drove my car back to Minneapolis and began work. Two weeks later I flew back to California, got married, stayed two days, went back to Minnesota, bought a house to live in and returned to California to get our combined family.

Three acres of land right on one of the lakes that even came with a beautiful old mahogany hulled Chris Craft boat, too late in the year to be of benefit just yet. But there was soon to be sledding down the hill and ice skating on the lake. Other than that there was little to say that was good about being there in the winter. Seeing the kids all bundled up, standing out in the snow waiting for the school bus was always disturbing. So were some of the nights that were so cold that the house, even with two furnaces and a fire in the fireplace, was too chilly to be comfortable in when the wind was blowing. Eventually spring came and by mid May the kids were fishing off our dock. The boat was also in the water and it wasn't long before they all learned how to water ski. Great fun for a while but by mid summer the lake became weed infested to the extreme.

And then there were the mosquitoes. Bad enough in the daytime but once evening came they rose up out of the lawn in droves, making it impossible to enjoy this otherwise scenic place which looked out over the lake. Beyond that, the house also had a bomb shelter in the basement because we were located in the upper end of tornado alley and spent several evenings jammed into this small space together when tornado warnings were issued. While certainly a change of location that got me away from my old home and all its memories, it definitely was not our concept of an ideal place to live.

Additionally, except for the salary increase, there was nothing very rewarding about my new job, either. The program I was hired to work on was put on hold by the government and for six months all we did was play a waiting game, staying busy doing little of nothing. That was bad enough, but then I was transferred into a section under a new boss who seemed threatened by my presence. That was when I called my old supervisor in California. Not only did he offer me my old job back, he also got the company to pick up all the moving expenses for the return trip so, a mere nine months after moving to Minnesota, we were back in California living in a brand new house and very happy to be there.

As for the new, old job I had returned to, it had been redefined. My boss had been promoted to a position where he would normally have sixty or more people under him and I and his one other direct employee would have had about twenty engineers each but for now it was just the three of us in a special projects group where we had status and technical challenge both, without the burden of personnel problems. As for my boss, he was a bit of a rouge and had his own way of dealing with things. A big aerospace company with thirty six thousand employees in our division alone, there were always lots of meetings to attend. Back then when smoking was allowed in the workplace and we were in a meeting that wasn't going where he wanted it to, he would take out a big cigar, light up and fill the air with thick smoke which almost always got people to wrap things up quickly.

The other thing that exemplified his approach to life was that he held what he termed our staff less, weekly staff meeting in a topless bar across town where we had lunch on the company and played a few games of pool before going back to work. As for home in our new neighborhood, it was the first and only time in my life where we had decent neighbors. There were four couples. Us, one next door and two across the street who we actually became good friends with and spent lots of evenings, weekends and holidays together. Unfortunately, at the same time on the personal level, things were beginning to go astray. It rotated around my wife and her mother. There were some minor indications of trouble in Minnesota, which instead of getting better once we returned to California, slowly got worse and it was then that I began to learn why.

Her mother was a verbally abusive, somewhat psychotic, one hundred percent bitch who went to great lengths to control my wife's father and her children. For one thing, if something went wrong she would go to bed and refuse to get up. Once she stayed there for a whole week until she got what she wanted. And wimpy man that he was, my wife's father would bring her meals and wait on her the entire time. In addition to that, my wife, the oldest child, had been subjected to some very serious verbal abuse from the time when she was a little girl right up into adulthood, none of which I ever began to find out about until after we were married. Therefore, my new wife, attractive and highly intelligent, came with a lot of heavy baggage that eventually got out of control and led to the end of our marriage.

As for my relationship with her parents, that was clearly defined right from the beginning. Having at least been told that her mother was difficult, we went to see her parents for the first time in their brand new house where we sat on their brand new couch where it quickly became clear that her mother could well be a problem. That more than obvious, I took a cue from from my boss at work, pulled out a cigar and lit up. Then I smoked the whole thing right in front of her parents, using the cuff of my pants as an ashtray while pretending not to notice the look of horror on her mother's face. And then when the cigar was down to a stub and no offer of an ashtray to put it in, I said it was time to leave.

Point made, in the dozen years I knew her parents, this nasty, bitchy woman never treated me with anything less than outright respect and never again criticized her daughter in front of me. Sadly, their behind the scenes relationship still remained an entangled love-hate situation my wife had extreme difficulty with, so much so that she tried to commit suicide on two occasions and became increasingly alcoholic in the end and turned to drugs some years later. Other than that we had three relatively normal years back in California before making another change.

MARYLAND

Mike was a man I had worked with a few years earlier in California. During that time he bought a monster motorcycle, took a short leave of absence and roamed around the back roads of Mexico, staying in little villages and out of the way places for several weeks before coming back to work. Then he got a job offer in Colorado and went to work for another hi-tech company on a spy satellite program. Once there he sold the motorcycle, bought a jeep and spent all his spare time camping out up in the mountains stalking big game. Another year later and he was in Maryland where he was now the vice president of yet another hi-tech company, this one smaller but with a range of leading edge programs and it wasn't long after that when he stopped to see me. He was visiting a new girl friend, this one the ex-wife of an undercover cop in Newport Beach. I didn't get to meet her then but he got to meet my new wife and said to come back and see him sometime when convenient. Then he gave me a packet of write-your-own airline tickets which were available back then before all the heavy traffic, the need for reservations and all those other restrictions.

At least a month went by before I even considered any of it but then, there I was at Dulles Airport where he picked me up. Not alone, this time, his California woman had moved back to stay with him. But not in a house or apartment. He was living on a boat instead, tied up in the harbor in Annapolis on the Chesapeake Bay. Not an ordinary boat either. It was a steel hulled monster that he had gone to Holland to buy and had sailed back across the Atlantic by himself. No longer an outdoors-man, he was now a seaman, along with something else.

The something else that was also readily apparent was his style of dress. He often wore a fringed, deerskin jacket and carried a fringed, purse like satchel hung over his shoulder and, thanks to his new hippy like lady friend, had been introduced to smoking pot. And so was I. Only later and in a more unorthodox manner.

Once again it was one of those opportunities that were hard to resist. Another raise in pay plus stock options, or an even bigger raise in pay and no options. Although this small hi-tech company of about thirty people was promising, I took the money instead of options and we moved to Maryland, not too far from the nation's capitol. Maybe if we could get far enough away from my wife's mother, things would be better at home also. But what had I gotten into?

Two weeks on the new job, and before my wife and family was able to come east, the company president invited me to a party at his house. Twenty people sitting in a big circle on the living room floor was hardly my definition of a party, however. At least not when they were all smoking pot, passing joint after joint around. No, but thanks, I must have said more than a dozen times that night as no one seemed to mind while I looked them all over. A few soon layed back and fell asleep. One guy started laughing hilariously to himself. Another little group stared arguing about how to conduct a street demonstration. Others just seemed to ramble. The company president and his wife started necking with each other and before long I made my excuses and left. Fortunately, I was never invited back and the subject was never broached. Later, as a point of interest only, I learned the way the president had gotten his job was to mortgage his house and use the the money to buy a large enough block of company voting stock to get himself elected. Well, why not, I said to myself. Except for his definition of what constituted a good time, the man was actually far from stupid. Not a bad boss, either.

The title I was giver was Operations Manager, third

man down from the top, but the job had nothing to do with company operations. Instead, it seemed that in addition to writing new business proposals for advanced state-of-the-art military equipment, I had been hired to get some programs back on track that had originally been given to the president's younger brother to run which he had stalled out on. Meantime, one of the fringe benefits of the job was having an office adjacent to my old friend Mike. Among his other talents, Mike was also a woodworker and a talented guitarist and the first thing he did after his girl friend went back to California was to stay up many nights and handcraft his own guitar, piece by piece. Then he and one of his employees would sit in his office and play classical tunes during their very long lunch hours. Other than that Mike and I played an occasional game of pool together but our relationship was of no further significance regarding work or in my personal life and I have only mentioned him because of his unique individuality, something I have continued to do regarding other people in other parts of this book also, for no other reason than that of their individual significance to me at the time.

Then, on the personal side away from the job, we bought a large twin engine boat that slept six people and spent many weekends fishing, crabbing and exploring the Chesapeake Bay. Other than that we visited all the many attractions of the capitol and the area. The museums, national monuments, places of interest, the many good restaurants, went to New York City and Niagara Falls and things went fairly well for quite a while. My wife also got a job to stay busy and we settled into our suburban home. But, all in all, what did any of it matter. Our marriage was continuing to deteriorate and two years later we were back in California again. More job changes and career moves.

Manager, new programs department, chief engineer,

executive VP and small company CEO. Technical challenges, company politics, a wife with deep emotional issues, children in an increasingly difficult situation. Then, finally my three children were through high school and out of the house and I'd soon be fifty. It was more than time to go our separate ways. We didn't get angry and fight about it or hire attorneys, however, we negotiated instead.

But there was no big party to celebrate once the divorce was granted. Instead, all those left behind years seemed regretful, sad, confusing, and I was extremely lonely at first. No outside job to go to, I had started a small business and was working out of my garage at the time. Alone. I had no close friends, my parents lived too far away and had their own difficulties and if it hadn't been for the fact that my ex and I had stayed friends and still spent a lot of nights together, I'm not sure how it would all have turned out. With that said, some of which is repetitive, that part of my story has gone full circle and I return to the point where I was living in Arizona.

The first house I lived in was in the uptown area of Sedona. It was where I continued my relationship with Dee, met Roy, Two Birds and a lot of other people and it was in that time period where the woman named Midge disappeared. After six months I moved to a house half way up the mountain on the way to Jerome which I shared with a woman I had met in a local poetry group. There I continued to do a lot of hiking, met the woman Carol who lived out in the canyon for six months and sat down and wrote two novels which could have been sequels to some of Edward Abbey's books. By the time the half year lease on the house was up, however, my just a housemate, had left and gone back to San Diego., making the place unaffordable for me alone. As a result I put all my possessions in storage and lived in my truck for about seven months before renting a place in the Rimrock area for six more months.

Then, somewhere in there it began to rain and I went back to living in my truck again and once in a while I would stop and spend a few nights with my old friend Dee who now lived in a ground floor apartment on a small island in the middle of Oak Creek. That February it rained for 21 days straight. Towards the end of that period it came down even harder. In two days the creek rose over sixteen feet and threatened to overflow the island and by three in the morning on the second day we evacuated whereupon the force of the water took out the door of her apartment and left half a foot of mud and debris behind.

The flowing water also washed out a couple of minor bridges downstream, completely destroyed a trailer park along the creek, carrying whole trailers with it along with uprooted trees, old barrels, trash and more, even an automobile with a woman in it who made the mistake of trying to cross the raging water a ways up the canyon. The "one hundred year flood" as they described it. Except it didn't just happen once in a hundred years. It happened two years in a row, with the following year being just as bad.

Maybe it was even worse but it was hard to compare because by then I was living in another house along the creek in the Page Springs area, six or seven miles downstream from the Sedona area but this one was high up above the creek bed and far safer. Even so this minor waterway, which was normally about ten or twelve feet wide, rose in depth to the point where it spread out five or six hundred feet in the area below the house and raged and roared for days on end. Again it ripped out trees and parts of people's buildings, a few more trailers and everything else that got in the water's path but the one hundred year old, remodeled schoolhouse I was staying in with a new woman friend remained dry and intact up at the top of the high bank it sat on. As for the relationship with this person I will call Susan, that was a different story.

It started out well enough. We liked each other and after a couple of months I moved out of my truck and into her house. In addition to paying her a modest amount of rent, I also remodeled her kitchen and an old cabin that sat on the eight acre property, built a garage and a carport, trimmed all the trees and mowed down all the weeds and brush that over-ran the place. Then I chopped a lot of firewood we used in the old stove in the winter and burned in the fire pit out back where we had many drumming sessions and a few weekend encampments the rest of the time.

We swam in a large pond the creek had created, ate outside in the evenings and enjoyed the abundant wildlife. Javalena would come by as night approached, little babies tagging along. Fearless baby skunks would also show up and walk right under the table where we sat, looking for a morsel. Then there were racoons who would look in the window after dark and try to get into the container where we kept the cat food, even stealing the large plastic bin itself one night when we were asleep.

Other than that there were large numbers of birds, a band of coyotes, a few mule deer, an occasional red fox, some very big rattlesnakes, a mountain lion down by the creek that would wake us up with it's god awful scream and an infestation of scorpions in the house that resisted all attempts to do them in. Having been stung more than a dozen times, on the leg, foot, arm, hand, neck and more, the important thing to remember is that no matter how horrible the pain, the venom is not going to kill you, seeking medical help is a waste and the agony will eventually turn into a numbness that will finally fade away.

As for my housemate, although we did have some interesting times of our own, she was not a good person to get very emotionally involved with. For one thing she had a lot of unfinished business with an old boyfriend from back in California where she had previously lived. For another we seemed to be limited as to how we were able to connect intellectually. Regardless, even though we spent at least half of our time going our separate ways, we still shared her house together for over eight years.

She made three different trips to California to spend time with this man from her past and he made two to Arizona before she finally realized what a muddled individual he was. At the same time I made many trips back to California myself to visit my one daughter and my son, along with an old girlfriend named Barbara, a portion of whose story I also include. Additionally, I made the cross country trip I described earlier, drove to the Denver area several times to visit my sister and roamed the many back roads of Arizona and New Mexico, sleeping in my truck along the way.

I also visited Two Birds in New Mexico several times, did the vision quest there and participated in native American ceremonial gatherings, made one last trip to Europe and another to Australia. And then, there I was one day wondering how many free airline miles I had left from all the flying I had done and where I might go to use them up. What about Peru and Machu Pichu? That is where this whole story began. Don't go to Peru. Don't go anywhere that isn't across the street from a good hospital, you could drop over at any moment. Especially, don't go to Peru or any place that high up. If nothing else does, the high altitude will kill you for sure. So I didn't go to Peru, I came to Arizona instead. And even though that was six years ago, seeing all those old Inca ruin sites was still something I really wanted to do. But should I?

I had stopped taking all the prescription meds I was supposed to be on for the rest of my life and except for exercise, I hadn't done one thing the doctor had ordered in a very long time. So now what, I wondered at the time and almost immediately told myself, why even bother to ask because I still might not like the answer so don't get stuck there. The more important question was, did I have enough miles to get to Lima? The answer was no. But I did have enough to get to Quito, Ecuador and that was right next door to Peru. Sort of. Only about another thousand miles to Lima. I could figure that part out later. So, ticket in hand, I went to the airport.

And once in Quito, how did I feel? Back in Arizona the first time I drove up the canyon to Flagstaff I had to turn around before I got there because my chest began to hurt. I was also having difficulty breathing and it took a couple of nitro pills to get me back down the mountain. But the altitude at Flagstaff was only seven thousand feet. Quito was more than ninety three hundred and what a surprise when I got off the plane. I could breath easily. Remarkably so. And even though Cuzco would be another two thousand feet higher than that, my fears began to dissipate because so far the thin air actually felt good.

With that concern largely behind me, I spent the first night in Quito, then started riding buses around the country, visiting towns and villages for nearly a week. Then, after two more days and nights in Quito I went to Riobamba and got up at three a m the next day to catch an old meandering train down the west side of the Andes mountains to Guayaquil, nine thousand feet to sea level in ten hours. A short train, eight cars in all. Four were for passengers, two were full of gravel which was dumped on the roadway half way down, and two diesel engines. The passenger cars could hardly be deemed first class because they were actually old, doorless boxcars with wooden benches nailed to the floor down the middle. It was where the definitely overcrowded passengers all sat until the sun came up. Then the majority of them climbed up onto the roof of the moving cars and sat where the view was much better, men, women and children alike, no complaints from the train crew.

The following day a flight from Guayaquil to Lima. A night sleeping in a chair at the airport, then on to Cuzco, altitude eleven thousand two hundred feet where many of the tourists were buying and chewing on coca leaves because of headaches and altitude sickness. Not me, however. I spent three days walking the town, enjoying the natives, eating food cooked on little charcoal grills along the street, went up the hill behind the town to explore the ruin site at Sacsahuaman and finally got on the train to Machu Picchu where I spent three nights in the on-site hotel. A good choice because in the evenings the majority of visitors were gone, leaving the ruin site to be explored in depth without all the people and their chatter about how all this was possible. But just like Sacsahuaman and many other sites around the world where multi ton monster stones have been carved and moved, how was it possible?

How did ancient people get multi ton boulders up and down and back up steep mountain sides, shape them and put them in place? Conventional explanations simply do not apply and for me it was something to keep pondering over. I also took the challenge and climbed a small, almost straight up cone shaped peak about five hundred feet high adjacent to the ruin site just to see if I could do it. Then it was re-trace my steps, return to Quito and on to Arizona after nearly a month, mission accomplished, feeling absolutely great physically. Seeing parts of other cultures that were still largely intact in the rural areas had also been very rewarding. Seeing gaunt, ragged little children sent into the airport to beg for money, however, was always heartbreaking. But instead of giving them money, I preferred to take them to the sandwich bar instead and let them pick out whatever appealed to them.

Except for one tiny, unwashed, underfed little girl in tattered clothing, however, about six or seven years old in Lima. She tugged on my pants leg and looked up at me with the biggest, darkest, saddest eyes I have ever seen. Eyes that seemed without hope. Eyes that stunned me so much I could only stare back and failed to react quickly enough before she moved on and lost herself in the crowd. Eyes that still haunt me sometimes when I remember that trip and still bring tears to me own in this unjust world where such things should never be allowed to happen.

Anyway, about a month after I returned home I went to California to visit some family and out of curiosity, stopped in to see our old family doctor and told him about my medical history, leaving out the part about throwing away my meds and not following the cardiologist's orders. With that he took me into an exam room and ran an EKG. Well, he said after he looked at the data, if I had ever had a heart attack, there was absolutely no longer any evidence of that ever having happened. Except that it had in a very extreme way which, after hearing what he had told me, led me to the conclusion that listening to my own inner voice instead of following the cardiologist's instructions had been the right decision after all. As for Susan, that was a different story.

In addition to all the work I did at her house I also found time to write four more books. Three novels and a non fiction work, knowing all the while that I should also be looking for a different place to live. Not another rental property. That would just keep draining away my resources. Unfortunately, I couldn't afford to buy either. I'd have to find a decent job and go back to work to do that, something I wished to avoid if at all possible. Besides, I was nearing seventy and chances of finding anything financially meaningful at that age seemed slim. That being the case the only alternative left seemed to be to get a piece of land and pitch a tent on it, or get a trailer and over time, build my own house and with that in mind, I went searching. That search even took me up into Colorado and southern Utah.

Kanab, in particular interested me because of it's spectacular natural beauty, as did other parts of that area even though they had some major disadvantages from my point of view. The primary one was that those people had religion. I did not. And most certainly I was not a Mormon so socially it might be difficult. Additionally, the area was just too far from any town or city of any real size and all the rest of the people I still had left in my life. Regardless, I drove there several times, camping out in my truck while checking out the social aspects of the situation. This entire search for another place to live went on for nearly two years. What I liked I couldn't afford and what I could afford I didn't like. Then one day I was driving down Loy Road in Cornville for no particular reason and there it was. A real estate sign on the west side of the road in front of a very steep, completely undeveloped hillside property. No road up the hill. Nothing. I parked and walked to the top. Six acres of land and what a view. This had to be it.

New home site acquired, I started by talking to a man named Emmit. Emmit was a tall, lean, tough old man who was pushing eighty pretty hard but had three ancient bulldozers, a backhoe, a dump truck and two full sized road graders and lived in an old shack of a house on several acres of land down the street that looked like a combination auto junkyard and city dump. The steep hill on my new property, however, seemed to challenge him for some reason and without agreeing on a price he brought his biggest dozer down and started in, first building a strong wire fence half way down the side slope so rocks wouldn't roll out into the road. Then he started pushing dirt and small boulders around, usually only working a half day at a time because, after all, it was July. Eventually he made it up the first slope, around the corner and clear to the top where the house would be in spite of two major interruptions. Monsoon rainstorms which washed large amounts of dirt down the hill and out onto the road.

This upset the county road department quite a bit because they had to come and clean it up but we got through it and though it was not exactly a street, my new driveway was at least passable when it wasn't raining. As for Emmit, all I could do was hand him a check for a few hundred dollars every so often until one day he refused the one I offered and said that was enough, he was happy. So was I. If I had hired a contractor instead, it would have cost me at least four times more than it did. Plus we became friends of sorts. He even came over once with his tractor to rescue me when I got the old backhoe I had later bought for myself in a precarious situation where I could have lost it over the side of the hill.

At the same time Emmit was working his way up the hill with his bulldozer I had gathered information from the county building and planning department and the library and began designing my house to be. And while I couldn't afford to make it exotic, it had to be my house and my plans, not something I bought a ready made set of but at least somewhat customized to the site and my personal needs. In the process I pounded a lot of stakes in the ground at Susan's house, laying out floor plans to check dimensions, locations of doors and windows and other aspects, then made an acceptable set of drawings for the house and a large storage shed and got them approved. Then I negotiated a cash deal with a well driller, bought a used cement mixer and built my shed while he pounded a one hundred fifty foot hole in the ground. That done with a casing down into what appeared to be an underground stream, I poured a slab, put the pump, pipe and wiring down the hole and built a well house which then led to the next steps in this multi phased project. How to get the water four hundred feet up the hill to the house location and how to get electricity five hundred feet from the road up the hill to the house and back down to the well. No matter what else, at least the water pipes would have to be underground. And what would that cost? A lot. Too much in fact and it was then that I remembered seeing a sign along the freeway fifty miles away down by Black Canyon City for a used equipment yard.

Not even hesitating to think it through, I got in my car, drove down and there sat the solution to my problem. It was an old power company trencher which someone had brought in two days before with a blade on it that would go down six feet into the ground. Nearly impossible to get started, it's two cylinder diesel engine was only running on one but I made a low cash offer, went home and got my trailer and brought it back and by noon the next day had it running strong as ever. And then the real work began.

The first trench that had to be dug was from the power pole near the street below up to the top of the hill nearly six hundred feet away and it had to be at least five feet deep according to the power company and would be along the edge of the upper driveway. Ordinarily this might not have been such a difficult job except that the hill was not composed of dirt, it was alternating layers of sand and rock with most of the rock layers being thicker than the trencher blade was long which meant grinding through solid rock in several areas going up the hill.

In the sandy portions it was possible to extend the trench twenty or thirty feet in one day. But when it came to the rock, the old machine would snort and belch black diesel smoke, jump up and down and grind away, sometimes taking over an hour to go only a foot. What made things even more difficult was the fact that it was also far too dangerous to operate the machine sitting in the seat as it backed down the hill so I had to walk along beside it and operate the controls from there, always ready to disengage the clutch on the big cutting chain so the engine wouldn't stall out.

Additionally, the controls were on the side of the machine that forced me to be on the very edge of the driveway next to the side slope as it ground away, bringing up dirt, dust and an occasional rock that it would kick out and roll down at me. Eventually, however, after wearing ear plugs and breathing exhaust fumes for six weeks and some other equipment difficulties, I finally finished the trench for the primary electrical service. Then I had it inspected and put in the several hundred feet of conduit and filled up the long slot in the ground.

Then it was time to put in another trench down the middle of the driveway for the water pipes and the electrical service back down the hill to the pump house, a much easier task since that one only had to be three feet deep. And finally, one last trench on the other side of the driveway only two feet deep for the sewer pipe from the septic tank down to the drain field which would be in the area by the storage shed. Next job, move about a hundred tons of dirt and rock up top to make the pad for the house big enough to put a building on. That, of course, required a tractor-backhoe which I didn't have either. Again, the same problem as with the trencher. Hire a contractor, rent one or hope I could find a used one that was affordable.

After looking at two different machines that I thought were grossly over priced, I got in the car, drive down to Black Canyon City once more and just like with the trencher, there sat an old monster of a machine that the owner had taken in two days before. More serendipity. About thirty years old, it needed a lot of minor attention but still ran very well. Taking out a roll of hundred dollar bills, we negotiated and after working on it for a few days making repairs after I got it home, it was ready to go and once again, like the trencher, it saved me several thousand dollars in the end. I used it to make the house pad and extended the parking area, dug the deep trench for the drain field, extended and widened the lower driveway and a lot more. Then the trencher went back to work to carve the trenches for the house footings out of what was again, mostly rock.

At this point it is not my intent to burden the reader with the entire, strung out process of building my house, step by step. What is somewhat significant is the fact that with the exception of putting down the concrete slab for the house which required some help, I did every bit of the rest by myself. That included putting about three thousand cement blocks in place for a two story, twenty six hundred square foot building, doing the plumbing, electrical, floor tile, cabinetry, roof, paint and all the rest which ultimately proves very little.

Many other people would be capable of doing the same thing if they wanted to badly enough. What it took was determination and perseverance. And in my case, necessity, because doing all the work myself was the only way I would be able to afford what I ended up with. And what I ended up with was a house with a view and enough land to give me a great deal of cherished privacy and control over my personal space. Additionally, when the final inspection approval was issued, I was seventy five and in better physical condition than I had been in twenty years. Beyond that I was constantly intrigued with what can only be called the serendipity factor as things moved along. That was learning to sometimes set logic aside and listen to that little voice that nudges you to do things your common sense says are meaningless.

Not only did I find the two pieces of heavy equipment I needed when I needed them, this, call it luck if you want, spilled over into lots of other areas also. Purely by accident, if you will, I also stumbled onto several hundred cement blocks for half price from two different people, several hundred feet of rebar for free, an expensive kitchen sink for one dollar, a huge bathroom mirror for ten dollars, enough plywood for the entire roof at a sell out price, and on and on, these things always showing up at the right point in time.

Take the old tractor/backhoe I had acquired for example. After many hours of use that saved me a lot of money, worn out bearings in the differential finally gave way and destroyed all the teeth on the ring and pinion gears, requiring replacement of the entire unit. But new parts were no longer available and a used differential sold on the internet cost more than a thousand dollars, plus shipping and handling.

Now what, I asked. Even if I paid the price it would take at least a week to get it and I couldn't wait that long. Backtracking, checking the metal tag on the unit I saw it was made by Rockwell. Rockwell, as I knew, made rear axle assemblies for large trucks. Calling the only truck wrecking yard within driving distance I was told they had no such thing. Then, that little voice. There was an auto wrecking yard down the road about ten miles. My logical mind, however, said don't bother. All he has is cars and small trucks like pickups. I knew that, but without calling ahead, I went there anyway.

Knowing the owner, I told him my problem. He looked at me oddly for a second then pointed out the window of his office. There, blocking one side of his parking area was what was obviously a truck rear axle, two old rusty wheels with flat tires still attached.

"Some dumb ass dumped it there in the middle of the night, last night," he said. "I have no idea what it is off of but if you can use the damned thing you can have it for getting it out of my way."

I went outside and looked at it. Old and beat up as it was, it still had a tag on it that said it was a Rockwell unit, although not the same number as on mine. But still, I pondered, went home, got my trailer and hauled it off. As I soon found out after taking it apart, the differential gear box was the same as that in my tractor, the only difference being that the axle shafts on the truck unit were longer than those on the tractor which accounted for the different tag number. But, they were the same diameter, however, and had the same number of splines on the shaft. Thus, with the exception of having to drill two of the twelve mounting bolt holes in a slightly different place, this new differential fit perfectly into the rear end of the tractor and was actually in very good condition internally in spite of how bad it looked on the outside. So, somehow, by some quirk of fate, a very expensive and hard to resolve problem was fixed without cost, all in one day's time. Again, it was about not letting logic rule the moment, something I keep reminding myself not to do so much of anymore.

Regardless, after four and a half years the major challenges of home building were over and I was living in the house. But, it seems, that if you own the place, it's never done so over the next few years I mixed a lot more concrete, put down sidewalks, a patio slab out front, a much larger one in the side yard and another in the back which, with a roof, became a carport. Then I gathered up several large rocks and walled in the front patio area, built two different gazebos and experimented with a solar room on top of the house. And while all of that had its own significance at the time, it was still of secondary importance overall.

Even if I ever got to the point where I was willing to call it done I didn't want a series of on-going projects to fill up the days of my life and keep me distracted nor did I have the right mentality to be riding around in a golf cart and trading stories about what we used to do before we got too old to keep doing it. But I did like people. That was important and for several years we had what we called a "soup group" going. With five other couples and myself, every month we would go to one couples' house where, to keep it simple, the main course was their choice of soup, bread, wine and desert and then rotate to the next house the following month.

I did not have a significant lady friend at the time but usually found someone to invite if someone else didn't find someone for me. What was most important, however, was the fact that there were several very prolific and somewhat well know artists in the group who liked discussing controversial ideas. Then another couple was added to the group and our times together expanded into holiday affairs, birthdays and other occasions until several years later when one couple dropped out because someone else who sometimes drank a little too much wine offended the wife. Another couple then moved away, one good friend fought a losing battle with cancer and another had a minor stroke and descended into the world of dementia. Even so, there were other parties at my new house too and other people came and went, one of them being housemates who slept in my guest bedroom and shared the rest of the house.

This person was a psychologist and author who alternately spent six months in the U S and six in Switzerland. There she ran a school for other psychologists. She also had a house in Jerome when we first met which I helped her sell. The, when she moved in with me she brought along a large sofa, a dining room set, a bedroom set and lots of paintings, none of which I owned at the time. Two years later she met a man on line and got married, didn't need the furniture and left it all behind. More serendipity for me. As for other people who made a difference in my life I will now touch on some of them without regard to chronology or criteria. The fact that I chose to mention them alone serves to show their significance.

NAXIE

Not previously knowing each other, Naxie and I both showed up on the same day to check out a creative writing group at the local library. There it seemed, we had some kind of undefined connection that made us destined to become friends, something which became more apparent after the meetings when several of us in the group would gather at a fast food place near the library where I learned that the person I was dealing with was a complex, very intelligent, high IQ individual who was also a writer and published poet with two grown children who had divorced her husband after more than thirty years of marriage and was trying to re establish her life, first in Las Vegas and then in Arizona. Eventually, she gave up living alone, stored her furniture and stayed in my spare bedroom for several years before finally buying a home of her own. Now a most important best friend, she is very personable, has a quick sense of humor, makes friends easily and remains loyal to them over the years. Additionally, it seems that we rarely ever ran out of things to talk about. She is willing to both, ponder the universe and explore what greater meanings life may have to dealing with the smallest of everyday problems people encounter.

JOCELYN

It was just a small, two line ad in the Beverly Hills Courier.

Journaling   workshop. $50.00
Jocelyn Brando   555-1234

Sounded interesting, I thought, having no real idea as to what journaling really was. So was the name of the person giving it. Interesting, that is. Was she related to Marlon, I wondered. Couldn't be. But what did it it matter.

Jocelyn lived on an appropriately named street tucked away in a small hilly area in Santa Monica about three blocks from the beach. The exact part of the beach where Richard Bach always took walks on years before when the voice kept coming to him. Jonathon Livingston Seagull, Jonathon Livingston Seagull. It was something he kept questioning severely, never knowing what it was all about until many years later he sat down and out came the book by the same name, which he also swore he had no idea where it came from either.

At any rate Jocelyn lived on Rustic Rd in a tiny little house on this old tree lined street. She was probably about ten years older than I and what I wish for now is that I could visualize her face a little clearer after all these years but if I happened to hear her voice I would most certainly

171

recognize that. To say it was gravely would be a gross understatement.

It was a Saturday afternoon, six weeks course which she conducted in the garage behind her home. Not a garage any longer because it was one of the very few things Marlon had ever given her money for. Yes, he was her brother and the garage was converted into a two room studio which consisted of a library room and a small kitchen. The library side where she gave the course had floor to ceiling bookshelves along two walls and probably had more paper back books on them than the public library and she claimed to have read them all.

There were seven of us in her workshop. Seven times fifty is three hundred and fifty dollars and I'm sure she could well have used the money. The course was strictly Progoff, the accepted authority on the matter, work books and all but I found it to be very insightful and surprising as to where it led. Jocelyn herself was very intelligent, engaging and articulate with a hearty sense of humor, made most endearing by her raucous, raspy voice which most likely was helped along by her smoking, the only true chain smoker I ever met. When she smoked, which was nearly all the time, at least twenty cigarettes were lit off of each other, all in a row. Then, when the course was over she gave us all a small wooden acorn, the symbol of wisdom, as a graduation gift and we went our separate ways.

A couple of weeks after it was over, however, I called to thank her and asked her to lunch. And that became a kind of routine. Every other week I would drive over to her house and we would walk down the few blocks to a small cluster of businesses on Pacific Coast Highway and eat and talk at this little oddball restaurant. It was then that she told me she was depressed because she had been seeing the same psychoanalyst for eleven years and the man had recently died. Of course we spoke of other things too. Philosophy, people, life's events, a little about Hollywood and some of the films she had been in, but never about her famous brother. And then I moved to Sedona but I would write to her from time to time and always sent her a card at Christmas. She answered too, but her words were always limited to what she could get on a simple postcard, twenty three cents each at the time. Christmas was the same. Very simple, too. Greetings, Best, Jocelyn.

Always something to look forward to, this lasted for more than a decade until one year, not so long ago, no card. Going on line, I tracked her down. And so much for all those critical people out there. All those cigarettes and she only lived into her nineties but damned if she isn't on the list of some of the people I miss the most in those quiet moments when I'm alone.

MARY

Dr. Mary was a psychologist with a practice in Westwood, just off Wilshire Blvd in west L.A., an attractive, adept and very personable individual. She was also one of the brightest people I had ever met. Not as a patient but at a party and we were friends for a while. I looked forward to seeing her from time to time because it truly was an encounter. A challenging game, sometimes to be sure, like mental racquetball with ideas bounced furiously back and forth. Humor, too, but wry and subtle in her case and she was always knocking on wood whenever there was a reference to herself, just in case her luck should run out. She lived in a second story apartment that looked out over the marina and the coast line of southern California and it was always a pleasure to sit out on the deck in the sun and watch the big yachts coming and going.

We wrote a small book together once, too. A pithy social commentary for the singles world and missed the market by less than a month. Then she wrote another book, a near best seller and had appearances on both the Carson and the Letterman shows and to most people who knew her, both as a psychologist and author, she seemed the picture of success. Behind that facade, however, the role she played quite well, was something she couldn't always hide and as the friendship deepened, her true plight became more apparent.

Sadness would describe it best, I think, and a vast loneliness for lack of better words. A puzzled soul, lost in a search for meaning. Something beyond her intellectual and educational abilities to resolve.

At forty, Dr. Mary had never been married but she had instead, fallen in love with a married man, the one true encounter of her life, someone she wanted desperately to be with. It was his story, too, she claimed. She loved him and he loved her and maybe it was so because they had made a plan, Dr. Mary and the man whose name was Jack. He was in the process of a divorce, a verified fact. She had checked it out, she said, and they were literally days away from moving in together when Jack, damn him to hell for what he did, and damn him to hell for what he wasn't able to do because Jack, damn him, Jack dropped dead in the middle of the day on his way to Mary's house.

It almost completely destroyed her, she told me, and being lost beyond reason without a place to turn, she had closed her office, sold all her possessions and began to travel. Wandered, would better describe it because her journey was totally without plan. Aimless and devastated, no goal in sight, hoping perhaps that somewhere in between, somewhere along the long lonely road, she might bump into someone or stumble over something that would help her find some meaning and show her the way back. But she never did.

Futile, was the way she described it. Running, running, running away from the ghost of her tragedy. No safe place to hide, no soothing arms to hold her. Always nothing, she said. Nothing but the distractions of rambling, meaningful only in their ability to divert her from pain. Some of the time at least, but never enough. Europe, Asia, Africa, South America, everywhere almost except the United States. She would be out there still, riding on a train or a bus, a ferry boat, a plane. Going somewhere, anywhere, she confided. It didn't really matter. At the time anything was better than dealing with her shattering, indescribable loss.

Regardless, in the end, what? It all came down to money. After more than five years she was penniless. Forced to return, she came back to Los Angeles, borrowed from a friend, reactivated her license and started a new practice and by the time I met her she was largely re engaged in life. Or so it seemed. But the sadness was still there. She couldn't always hide it and slowly she shared some of it with me. Then, for reasons I no longer remember, we drifted apart. I hadn't seen her in several years until one day, walking down the street in mid town L.A. I accidentally ran into her and said hello. We talked a bit. She had moved into a downtown highrise so she could be near the music center, the opera center, the theaters and the clubs, a different, cosmopolitan lifestyle and pretended to be happy about it. But truthfully, when I looked into her eyes and beyond the smile, I knew little had changed. The old sadness was still there and it broke my heart a little, just as it always had. Except that now, due to my own subsequent experiences, now I understood a little more about how she felt because during that interceding time I, too, had traveled the world and knew what it was like to never want to come home again. To be perpetually distracted. To remain apart, separated from the irreversible, only to learn that in the end that it is, above all else, asking too much. It is still impossible. Fortunately for me, however, I had run out of money much sooner than she, which brought me home in time to see the futility of what I had been trying to do. Doctor Mary never did, I don't think. Not completely, anyway. She still wandered, still a little lost in her waiting. That is what the smell of bourbon on her breath told me, along with the desolate look in her eyes. Waiting, I am sure, for the day when she could reunite once again with her lover Jack.

ANN

She was named after the first full month of spring and though she was approaching middle age at the time there was still a freshness and newness about her that was hard to resist. I met her at a penthouse party in the marina, unaware of what her background had been and it took a bit of catching up before I got it. Meanwhile I found out that she gave the wettest, sloppiest kisses a man could ever imagine and regularly cooked a spaghetti diner for her friend Cary Grant and eventually I connected the thought of purple shadows and garden walls with her name. She also knew a lot of people in the music world and one day decided I should meet one of her friends in the business.

Her friend Ann lived up at the top of a steep hill behind the Beverly Hills Hotel, two doors from a prominent psychoanalyst and across the street from some aging movie stars. The house she lived in came with her divorce but she remained friends with Manny, her ex, who still came by to help when something needed fixing. Manny owned a furniture store in Beverly Hills and they had been married for nearly twenty years before she met a songwriter who had come up with a major hit. She also found out that he had something else her husband was short on but didn't realize it until she stepped over the line and ended up in divorce court. In the end it wasn't the other man, however, as much as it was the tantalizing affect and the feel good fallout that came with her surreptitious behavior. Then, added to that, as she soon found out, she too, had a hidden talent that came to life in the new world she had indulged in.

This woman was bi-racial and when it came to appearance, she was a combination of the best of both. She also had a devilish sense of humor and a determined way of getting other people to adore her and seek her out and many were the impish games she played. She also told me on more than one occasion that she had the right to be quirky, unpredictable and irrational because she was a very creative person and any bad behavior on her part should be excused accordingly. Well, she most certainly was creative because there on her very large living room walls were over two dozen gold LP records along with a few platinums with songs she had written which had been sung by every major singer from Sinatra to Tom Jones and so much for that. I don't know that I was as impressed or overwhelmed as much as I was unable to put this kind of success in any kind of perspective I could understand so it was just out there as a part of her life but not of mine. The other thing I didn't understand was her occasional need to let me know which men in her life thought she had a great ass, especially when we were out and about and one of them said hello, usually a face I would recognize from a movie or TV show.

Besides that Ann was very entrepreneurial and rented out her spare bedrooms to aspiring actors. She also gave away some free mileage on her living room couch to her friend Julie who spent a lot of time hanging out at the Playboy Mansion and would tell us stories about her quickie escapades in the men's bathroom. Julie's need for the couch, however, was on ongoing affair she was having with the owner of a big Beverly Hills modeling agency who didn't want to be seen at Julies apartment complex or in a more public place. Julie was also a switch hitter and told more stories about macho actors who had performance difficulties but loved watching two women do their thing instead.

Ann also had put together her own cable TV show and sometimes used it to help clients she had acquired who had products to sell or a restaurant to promote. On two occasions she asked me to be the host because she thought I was a great interviewer but when people started coming up to me on the street afterward to say hello, I decided it wasn't the kind of career I wanted. Regardless, Ann's major interest was in putting together a weekly TV show which should have been picked up by one of the networks because of its uniqueness, but wasn't. Previously there had been a popular show called, What's my line? which had a panel who tried to guess the career of the guest who appeared, based on a minimum of actual clues. Her show also had a panel of experts but they were all of a different sort. An astrologer, a Tarot Card reader, an aura reader and a kinisthetic, a person able to pick up information off of a personal item of another such as a set of keys. She also wanted a psychic or two and with that in mind we set out to find some.

Using that as an excuse we went from psychic fair to psychic fair and were able to get dozens of free readings each, letting the reader know they might end up on TV if they were any good. But, there were none to be found so she went with what she had and started filming demos. Meanwhile she was also in search of a known celebrity as a host and even Leslie Neilson came up to the house to give it a try. Three years later, however, the whole thing had run its course and she finally gave it up but in the interim she had made dozens of new friends who would drop in and participate in some of the raucous parties she gave. She also stayed in touch with Jimmy, the kinisthetic, and when we all went to Vegas onetime we found that Jimmy was very good at walking up and down the aisles of slot machines and telling us which one was ready to hit. Beyond that she belonged to the Film Academy and we got to see a lot of pre-release movies and other friends gave her open invitations to charitable black tie events. The best of times, however, was when we bought a whole roasted chicken and a big box of fried rice and put it on the table and the psychoanalyst and his wife come up the hill and we picked it apart as we talked. We also went complimentary, to their weekend intensive, relationship workshops which were popular at the time but they were hardly trans formative as far as our own relationship was concerned. It was an, on again, off again, hit and miss affair that lasted several years. She was also a good friend to my son and spent a lot of time on the phone talking to my ex wife. Ultimately, however, I can only say that in all honesty, my feelings for her were very ambivalent, something which traced right back to the beginning.

I can still see her sitting there on our very first meeting looking back at me. Her dark eyes flashing, the little smiles that came and went and that almost teasing attitude that she projected outward as we talked and I remember viewing her with great curiosity, feeling that somehow I already knew her when I didn't know her at all. Even so, that sense never went away. As a person she could also be charming and attentive, extremely witty, provocative, taunting, sarcastic and critical all within the course of a few minutes while behind it all a nagging familiarity that often left me wondering. Who was this person? Why does she seem so familiar? And then, finally an answer. One kind of answer anyway, which could seem to make sense if it was possible to accept.

Ann had another friend, too. One I didn't get to meet until later on. This lady was from back east and only came west about once a year to give readings for a list of ongoing clients which included some well known movie stars and I have to say that until then, she was the only truly psychic person I had ever met. Needless to say, she gave me a long reading which included a list of very factual things which Ann didn't know and couldn't have told her. She also gave me an explanation of what was at the heart of my relationship with Ann which made a lot of sense in the context of a past life encounter, if one is willing to go there. At any rate, that did nothing to change our relationship. What brought it to a harsh end instead was the day I found out that she had been buying my ex wife drinks and plying her for information about our previous sex life. Where does one go after that? Regardless, recently divorced as I was at the the time, this woman was very good for me. She was always attentive, flattering, fun to be with and introduced me to a whole new world of people and events that I had never experienced before and I will always be appreciative of that.

BORIS

Another woman I met named Carla had divorced a top surgeon in the LA area. Not only did she end up with the big house in Brentwood but also the stretch limo they had shared. The chauffeur didn't come with the package, however, but that didn't matter because her new boyfriend was now behind the wheel. Usually she sat in the front beside him but once in a while she would sit way in the back as they made their private game of it just for fun. Carla's house was also the perfect party place. Big back yard, swimming pool, rec room with a pool table and wet bar. And that is where I met two people of interest. One was a guy named Boris, the other a woman named Sari. The relationship with Sari was not one to be discussed in public but as for Boris, he was different. Boris loved attention and that night he was holding down the pool table, taking on all comers. I didn't challenge him, however, but we talked later and became more than just acquaintances, but never complete friends.

Boris, as it turned out, was a Beverly Hills psychoanalyst who had a second floor office on Canon drive and truly fit the picture of what an analyst might and possibly should be like. In his forties, decent looking, sincere enough, impeccably dressed in the proverbial sweater and precisely trimmed dark beard, he fit the part well. He also loved to share his views on mental health and routinely invited others to his office and high rise apartment after hours to discuss theory of mind and other aspects of human personality. Mostly he targeted women as guests but if he felt you weren't going to make a move on any of his favorites, you were welcome as a man to help round things out.

While Boris's office was in a prime location, his apartment was on the wrong side of Doheney Drive, just across the street from Beverley Hills but it was elegant nevertheless. Boris had only lived there two years before I met him, however. Before that he had a private practice in San Diego and described his move to Beverly Hills as the most traumatic event of his entire life, something I had difficulty in understanding because by the time I met him I had had at least thirty different addresses behind me. At any rate one of the things I wondered about as far as he was concerned was that he had never been married or seemed to have a real girlfriend. And then I learned he had a different view of things, along with different aspirations. One that came into clear focus a little later.

It was on an evening when, lacking anything better to do, I dropped into Boris's office and found him still there, along with another friend of his and we decided to go for a drink at a bar over on Rodeo Drive, just a short walk away. Finally, after drink number three, the full story began to unfold. The two of them were collaborating on a plan. First, they wanted seven guys in all to make it affordable and share the adventure. Then they would go to Europe. Once there they would rent a tour bus. Using this vehicle they would visit every country in Western Europe. But first they would attach banners on both sides of the bus which declared them to be, The Beverly Hills Seven. Then they speculated on ways to inform the places they were going to visit in advance, hoping the allure of Beverly Hills would bring out someone to greet them. Women, of course. It was all about women. Hookers excluded, the final goal was for them all to have sex with at least one woman each, in every country they passed through before coming home. And then, with that presented in as enticing way as possible, they wanted to know if I wished to go along.

Good grief, I said to myself when they were done explaining it to me. What then? Once back home would we all sit down together and compare notes as to who had the most and best conquests? Well, no thanks but now at least I knew why Boris, eligible as he was, was rarely ever able to get more than one date from a woman before having to move on. What kind of psychoanalyst was this with his glorified idea of self and twisted way of viewing the opposite sex? Didn't he even see the kind of attitude he was revealing? No wonder most of his patients were men.

Well, needless to say, I declined, saying that I would

never be able to leave my job for such an extended period of time and that was that. So, enough drinking, they wanted to go eat. There was a good Italian place just down the street and around the corner, so we walked there and took a table in the back room. Except for a couple seated down at the far end, we were alone. The man just looked at us but the woman gave us a quick flash of a smile which Boris and his buddy didn't seem to notice and kept talking instead while I took another look. She was attractive enough, he not so much so and it soon became apparent that, even across the room, little things are given away. No rings on the fingers, she was out on a date with a guy she wasn't enjoying all that much, so I gave her a small hint of a smile back.

Many minutes later when we were about done eating, the woman got up and headed towards the women's room and only then did these two guys give her a look. Hmm, Boris said as they nodded their approval. Then, a few minutes later she returned. But this time she detoured slightly in her path, heading our way. It seemed too pat, such a thing couldn't ordinarily have happened. It had to have been pre planned to say the least. But no, nothing of the sort as she stopped and handed me a small note before returning to her date. Boris and his friend looked at me as I looked at the note. All it contained was a phone number and a first name. Janet. With that we divided up the check and left.

Who was that? Boris wanted to know outside.

Don't know her, I said with a shrug, thinking nothing could have been more appropriate and better timed. Two experts had shared all their opinions about how to succeed with women while the one who said almost nothing ended up with a phone number. Then, more questions. Was I sure I couldn't make the trip with them? And then, when we finally parted, Boris said that if I decided not to call this woman, could he please have the phone number?

Well, did I ever call her? No, because it was soon after that that I met another good looking woman at another party and ended up spending the next four plus years living with her instead. The one named Sharon I have discussed earlier.

JOYCE

From where I sat I could see at least two weeks of dirty dishes in the kitchen sink. There were clothes on the kitchen table and on the living room chairs, piles and piles of papers and printed material stacked in the corners and along the wall with what looked to be boxes of receipts, invoices, magazine articles, clippings and who knew what else. It was a good thing she didn't have a dining room table because there wouldn't have been room for it what with all the clutter. Not good. Maybe this would be a first and last date combined if this was any indication as to how she ran the rest of her life, I thought at first. At least until she came into the room, said hello and made me forget everything I had been thinking. A, happy to see me big smile, fresh faced, no makeup required, petite and sexy in a soft, silk print blouse and a trim, tailored dark skirt tastefully split at the sides, something totally different than the way she had been dressed when I first met her. Then a tiny wiff of what had to be an expensive perfume as she took my hand, said goodbye to her daughter and led me through the disaster of her house and out the door.

It was an after dinner date because she always had dinner with her daughter at home. That was good but the fact that she even had a child was not exactly a plus as far as I was concerned at the time. Regardless, at her suggestion, we ended up at the Disneyland hotel and took the outside elevator up to the top to the lounge and bar.

There we sat by the windows in the dim lit room with candles on the tables, looked out over the lights of Anaheim and had several drinks spaced out with lots of conversation that actually went somewhere. Conversation that also included a look at how brutally honest a person could actually be about things personal. Then, on the way home she asked if I would like to see her office and business.

She owned her own beauty salon, just a small one on the second floor in business center not far from her home, one that was in complete contrast to the way things were at her house. Up front a thick plush carpet on the floor, an expensive couch and a few chairs in the waiting area and two work stations in the back, all spotless and well organized. She even kept some candles in a drawer.

On our next date we went to country western bar with live music where she told me how much she loved Willie Nelson. And if she did, I was sure I could learn to like him too. Then, more dates and one day after about a month, one early morning actually, about seven a m the door bell started ringing and ringing. What the hell, I wondered as I woke up, found my robe and staggered out to the door. And there she stood with a seductive grin on her face. But only for a second. Without a word she stepped inside, shut the door behind her, took me by the hand, looked around and led me down the hall to where she knew the bedroom must be. There she shed her clothes and we climbed in together as she snuggled up close, made some quiet little sounds and almost immediately fell asleep.

It was on a Sunday, the salon was closed and it was her day off. But what prompted this? Was she making a surprise visit to see if I had another girl friend? Maybe, but so what and that afternoon we decided to go to a matinee movie. There was a long, slow moving line outside when we arrived which we joined. Waiting, she looked at me and asked another of the often blunt questions she sometimes came up with., "How many women have you had sex with?"

The girl in front of us must have heard it too because she hesitated in the line as it moved so I kept my voice low. Not knowing quite how to respond, I finally said that it was probably about the usual amount for a man my age, whatever that might be. And then what? Should I ask the same question in return? Did I really want to know? What difference would it make anyway? Well, unfortunately it slipped out as I foolishly asked her back.

With that she shrugged as if none of it were of any real significance and casually stated in a voice as ordinary and matter of factually as one might use to say two plus two equals four. "Maybe two hundred. After I left my husband. Before that, only two."

I looked at her. What kind of game was this? What was she trying to do? Shock me with such an extreme answer to see how I would respond? A test she was putting me to, perhaps? But no, that's not what the look on her face told me at all. My god! But by then we were at the ticket booth and then quickly inside. The rest of this would have to wait. Meantime what was the movie about? It was a new remake of "Sir Lancelot" which had come back around after many years and was all about brave men and pure and prideful women which was constantly being interrupted by my thoughts about two hundred guys and me, good old two hundred and one. If it was really true, her timing had been flawless. She had hit me with precisely when something deeper seemed to be emerging on my part. Had she done it intentionally? Why? Was it her idea of fairness to be telling the truth, the whole truth and nothing but the truth? For sure, it now seemed much too bizarre to be just made up game playing.

Now what, I wondered after the movie was out and we stopped for dinner. Was it time to kiss her goodbye and send her home? Should I be stopping at the clinic for a blood test first thing in the morning? Then what, I wondered because by then I was convinced it was the truth. Especially after the way she had shocked me on our first date during our evening in the lounge at the Disneyland hotel. There she had told me that a certain four letter word was her favorite word and not only did she love doing it but she also loved talking about it and liked to share her stories with some of her more open minded clients. So, if that was what our relationship evolved into, be informed. Much later, however, in spite of what she had said at that time, I found out that it wasn't that simple at all, being actually quite complicated emotionally and psychologically. Meanwhile all I could do at the moment was give myself time to consider just how important she really was to me so I left the entire matter alone and moved on from there. More country western music, some walks on the beach, the Renaissance Fair and on the times when she would drive up to my house in her shiny new, big black Cadillac we would walk across the street after dark and put down a blanket. Then we laid there looking up at the sky and had some very long conversations and it was then that I learned that all of her many escapades but one were one time only, quickie events, the reason for which soon seemed clear. The exception was an older man who had taken her on a couple of trips, a person she had no other interest in. And finally the question I had somehow never bothered to ask before.

"How long have you been divorced?" I wanted to know.

"I'm not," she stated. "But I've been separated for about five."

"Well," I said, considering that new bit of information,

187

wondering why it hadn't come up sooner.

"That's quite a while," I still responded as if that might have some importance, not knowing what else to say.

Then, for some unknown reason, taking things a little farther, I asked her if her husband had been the first man in her life. After all, she was the one who had first brought that subject up.

"No," she said. "He was the second. But he's the bastard that started it all."

I didn't ask her how, however. I just waited.

"I was pregnant and married at seventeen. He was nineteen and right after our daughter was born he started playing around. When I threatened to leave, he stopped and everything was pretty good until about five years ago when he started drinking a little too much and began staying out late once in a while. And, as if that wasn't bad enough, one night his buddy came over and they got drunk out of their minds. First he started insulting me and then the bastard wanted me to have sex with them both and this went on for quite a while so I finally told him okay but it would have to be his friend first and in private, pretty sure that by now his friend was far to drunk to do anything serious but I let him stumble into the bedroom anyway and waited, thinking that would really get to my husband later when he sobered up and thought the worst. Then I called the cops and they both spent the night in jail. A few days later he came by and picked up some clothes and I didn't see him for several months and it was more than a year before we began speaking again and worked out a visitation agreement for our daughter."

"What about now?" I asked.

"I'm not sure. For the most part I try not to go there but sometimes I think I still have feelings for him. Sometimes I even think I'm still in love with him, damnit. And maybe that's the problem. Somehow the love and hate of it got all mixed up. That and what with all the things about my father and I guess I lost sight of what was really important. I guess that's why I had so many affairs. I couldn't figure it out. Especially after the way our relationship started out."

"What do you mean?"

"He raped me."

"Your husband raped you? Before you got married?"

She nodded, pointing out that that was where their child had come from.

"But what's that got to do with your father?" he asked.

"He raped me too," Julie said.

"Jesus Christ," I said, overwhelmed.

"But he's dead now and there's nothing I can do about that. He died a long time ago. He was an alcoholic. He drank himself to death."

"I'm sorry," I replied, unable to think of anything else.

"Yes. Me too. In more ways than one but even that was too good for him. One day he came home after he had been drinking when my mother wasn't there, raped me and begged me not to tell her which I didn't because I thought she was too blind to see the truth and would never believe me anyway. Then a week later he did it again. Only this time he never said a word. Instead he took a gallon jug of vodka out to the garage, nearly drank the whole thing and died of alcohol poisoning before anyone discovered him there."

This time all I could do was to remain silent and wait.

"But that's not what's important," she finally said after some long moment. "Not any longer."

"What then?" I asked, still a little lost as to where to go from there.

"I'm not sure but finally, thanks to you, after being able to talk about it and be honest about with you and maybe a little more time, I think I might be able to forgive them both. Especially because of the way you accepted me for what I was. You never gave me a bad time or put me down or made fun of me. You just listened to me and accepted me without passing judgment and made me feel like a real person again. Whole. A really whole person. My father's dead and that is perfectly fine with me but my husband isn't and I hate to admit it even a little bit but I think I still love him. And he loves me too. I'm sure of that. And we have a child together who loves us both. I know it sounds crazy because he's kind of a simple shit in a way. Just a guy who got a bum rap from his parents as a kid just like I did and didn't know what he was doing half the time, just like me. But I think he's changed and now, I have too. Or at least I'm in the process and that's good. Isn't it?"

"Absolutely," I assured her. "It most certainly is."

That said we got up, went back to my house and got into bed, our only desire to spend the night holding each because somehow we both knew that this would be our last date together. Later, as time went by I checked up on her periodically. She did reunite with her husband and they were together until their daughter finished high school but soon separated afterwards and this time actually got a divorce. But that was it. I lost track of her after that, my own life taking other directions but looking back, oh yes. If she hadn't re connected with her husband I'm sure I would have been very happy having her in my life, past affairs or not. Or any of those other things that aren't really all that important.

<u>BRANDY</u>

Sometimes people do things that go entirely against the substance of who they are, thinking perhaps that it will somehow solve a problem but which catches them up in some greater entanglement instead, something even harder to escape from. And so it was for one woman I knew, an enigma unto herself.

A name, a fragrance, an event. One small thing tied to another, leading into the future, creating a story all its own. This one began in a most nebulous way with the new perfume my songwriter friend, Ann, wore one night when we went out to dinner a few years earlier. She thought it was distinctive and alluring and I guess I agreed. But while the aroma lingered, the rhythm of the name seemed to stick in my mind long after its essence had disappeared. Gengio. The newest cosmetic rage at the time and the chain of events that led from the name to the person who had first conceived of that name was long and sketchy. Eventually, however, it all came back to the fact that people lead you to people who lead you to more people in an expanding way and sooner or later you will meet someone you will have a special interest in. The other fact worthy of note is that while one of the keys to an upscale social life in a place like L.A. can come from celebrity status, it can just as easily come from money.

Take the Thallians, for example. The Thallians is a charitable organization that provides mental health services to thousands of people in the L.A. area who cannot afford private care and is supported entirely by donations. Over the years this particular charity has promoted itself into becoming a favorite of celebrities who like to be seen at its sponsored events, the annual grand ball and in print on the pages of the organization's publications. Every year they also select some noteworthy individual in the entertainment world to honor at another special event. The membership admission fee is, of course, a donation. And, if you can find a sponsor and are willing to write a check for the necessary amount, you can also become a member of the President's Club which gets you into some additional special events.

That being said, there I was, sponsored in, check

cashed, sitting amidst a sea of people all dressed in tuxedos and gowns, paying tribute to Carol Burnett, that year's guest of honor. Thallians president, Debbie Reynolds spoke, Ruta Lee, chairman of the board, spoke, others spoke, the orchestra played, we had a five coarse meal with wine and champagne and, dinner over, around came the ladies passing out the swag. Samples of expensive perfumes, lipsticks, those kinds of things for the women, and, an equivalent range of equally unimportant promotional items for the men. The woman who gave me mine was really quite cute, had a shy little smile and lingered just a bit before moving on. Later we danced together. I asked her, her name. It was Brandy and she gave me her phone number but it took a long time to put her whole story together and how she connected to a perfume named Gengio.

Fresh out of high school, Brandy came from Ohio to California looking for a job. Somehow she met the head chef of the Beverly Hilton Hotel, lived in a top floor apartment and had three children, a career-less housewife but with an enterprising mate. They started a cosmetic company with a special perfume as its foundation and she was the one who gave it its name. Gengio. And it started becoming successful, more successful than she had been made aware of. Then she caught him cheating and sued for divorce. Too soon, she should have waited a few more years. Then she would have benefited from a much greater windfall when the business was sold to major company for a staggering price. Regardless, he had full control of the money, did a good job of hiding most of it, spent a lot more on attorneys and judges, gained full custody of the children and cut her out of most of what she was due at the time. Complicating matters, she came down with guillain-barre syndrome and was alone and bed ridden for some several months. It was a desperate time for her, to be sure. The one significant thing she did have going for her, however, was the fact that she could well have been the real life model that the original Barbie doll was patterned after.

The time frame was shortly after the husband of a front page couple divorced his darling wife and started going with a mega movie star who then turned and dumped him. At any rate, Brandy met this husband shortly thereafter and went with him for a couple of years, on tour and elsewhere. Ultimately, however, the limitations of his manhood left Brandy unfulfilled and she moved on to affairs with some recognizable names in the movie industry. She had also acquired a billionaire boy friend from Austria who actually lived in one of the castles used in the movie, The Sound of Music. A married man with a lesbian wife who seemed to approve of Brandy. In addition to business interests in German and Austrian firms, the man also owned portions of some companies in the US and came to the States two or three times a year. When he did, he sent Brandy an airline ticket, some cash and the address of the hotel where he would be staying.

During the time I knew her and came to stay for my own weekends at her house, she was very open about that part of it. This included the fact that in addition to her get-away trips, this man also bought her a new, top of the line Mercedes and sent her checks for fifty thousand dollars on at least three different occasions as investment money, as well as a little something extra at Christmas. Well, fine. None of my business. Except why would I ever consider getting seriously involved with a woman who behaved like an expensive escort? That was one aspect of it. What was really aggravating about her was the fact that she felt compelled to tell me who else she had slept with when the occasion arose. Why, I am not sure but it seemed to be because she had the mistaken idea that that would make her look more desirable in my eyes. Something which it did not and only reflected how insecure she really was on a very basic level.

She had also acquired a few female friends along the way who seemed to keep very few secrets about their personal lives from each other. And, as she once explained, the most fun of all was comparing notes on the details of bedroom encounters with the men in their lives, something which left me feeling a bit off center when any of these women were around. But then, at one point she started dating a doctor she seemed to like a lot and introduced him to one of those same friends, the one who lived on the hill right behind her. But then, damn. One day after he left her house he went up the hill and knocked on her friend's door. Not only did her friend let him in, she took him down the hall to the bedroom and so much for that. A similar thing happened on another occasion also with a different man and that caused her to find some new girlfriends and change some of her standards.

One of the other things that was also very aggravating to her was the ingrained idea that people were prone to take advantage of single women in business dealings and this was one of several reasons she used for why I should stop messing around and step up and marry her. Somewhere in that train of events she also hired a contractor who tore down the garage where she kept the Mercedes, built a new one and added a very nice, self contained apartment above it. Once it was complete she told me that the reason she had done it was because, if I wouldn't marry her and live with her, she at least wanted me to come and live in the apartment so I would be nearby. Then, since that didn't happen, combined with her other recent experiences, she started dating a different kind of men. This I didn't find out about until the night when we were in bed together and the phone rang. She answered, put her hand over the mouthpiece and said, "it's my boyfriend", but not a word about wanting privacy or stopping what we were doing. Instead she talked to him in an endearing way and listened to him tell her how much he cared for her and ended by agreeing to see him two days later when I was gone.

"So, who was that?" I asked after she hung up.

She gave me his name and told me he was the manager of an upscale restaurant down on Rodeo Drive and the one really good thing about him was that he was totally impotent so she didn't have to worry about him cheating on her. Well, I suppose there was some distorted logic in that but she also informed me that she was on more than one singles site looking for a man to marry because she was tired of being single and this one was also too old for her. Then, a few months later, on another two day stop over at her house, she told me she had been successful in her search. She had found three qualified candidates for potential husband and had picked the one with the least amount of money and career success to go with and was seeing him regularly. Ten years younger than her, his name was Tom, retired from the service, a diabetic and also completely impotent. It was so totally bizarre I didn't even comment but it was the last time we were ever together again because she soon sent me a note saying she had actually married the guy.

Normally, that should have been the end of the story but, married or not, she still continued to e-mail me regularly. It all started out innocently enough, just the regular chit chat, old acquaintances staying in touch. Considering her situation, however, at any moment I fully expected to hear that she was separated, working on a divorce. Instead, the trivia she shared quickly turned into subtle erotica. For a while. Then erotica turned into things more explicit and full of innuendo and that in turn became downright pornographic, things I never directly responded to. Things which Dr. Phil would righteously have considered to be some form of infidelity all its own at this point. So, rather than encourage her I suggested she that if she was ever going to be happy, she needed a lover on the side instead. Maybe one of her old, more normal boyfriends who lived nearby that she could check into a motel with once in a while. Not me. I lived much too far away, I told her as an excuse when in fact I was just very definitely no longer interested.

Then, two other things happened in her life. First, her husband, had finally met her daughter who had come to visit from back east and it was devastating. He had totally and completely fallen madly in love with her, exquisite implants and all and told Brandyy about it in a pathetic confession. But, handicapped as he was, there was no place to go from there even if the daughter had been willing, which she was not. Brandy forgave him, however, in her own desperation, claiming she still loved him anyway and didn't want to lose him. Then he started digging into her personal computer, bringing up all the old e-mails to me she had forgotten to double delete, went ballistic and sent me a viscous message. There was no reply on my part, to be sure, and silence reigned for several weeks. Then, to my surprise, I got another e-mail directly from him. Not only was it an apology, it was also a proposition. The essence of it was that he now finally realized what a highly sexual being his wife really was and, since he was the way he was, it was probably in both his and her best interest if he allowed her more freedom. With that said he then made it very clear that it would be perfectly all right if the two of us rendezvoused from time to time because we had his permission. Well, okay. Thanks but no-thanks. I had already lost any desire to be with her even before she had married this person.

What ended any possible urge to pursue that side of our relationship any further was her confession about having a one time session with a TV newscaster. An older man who wore red suspenders to keep his pants up, had long stringy hair and looked like he hadn't been in the shower for weeks. But he had worn a condom, she had explained at the time as if that made it okay for her to rub bellies with this disgusting individual. I didn't say that to her husband, however, after he made his proposal Instead, I asked him if I took him up on the deal, was he going to come along and watch? A question which served its purpose because that was the end of any further e-mails from either of them and I largely forgot about her. That is until about seven years later when there was a message on my answering machine. Why I returned the call is still an open question. Just trying to be nice, I guess.

Anyway, Brandy's husband had died except that by then he was her ex husband instead. She had divorced him because he had stopped by to see an old girlfriend and, impotent as he was, had spent the night sleeping on her couch. But, for some reason that equated to infidelity in her mind and she put him out of her life. Then, her first husband, the father of her children, had also put himself out of her life for good, too.

He died two months later. Altzheimers. Fitting perhaps. But did it bring closure for her? The money he should have shared with her was gone and the fragrance had wafted away, but the memories had refused to depart and she was still bitter about that. Other than that she was still the same, impossible to have an in-depth conversation with person as always but with one significant difference. Instead of sending me more sexually explicit material she had warped over into the world of the ranting, right wing conspiracy extremists. Just like them, she seemed

197

determined to impose her new view of the world onto me by blitzing me with an unending series of these diatribes and seemed offended when I told her to stop.

I still get an e-mail from her once in a while, however. Just a short note about some difficulty she has encountered along with a short video clip of a field of wildflowers, some wild horses or some cute dog doing tricks. Things like that. Same old Brandy. In the more than twenty years that I have known her we are yet to have a serious sit down, in depth conversation of much of anything very important. I have tried because I'd really like to know what's going on in her head on a more fundamental level but she has always seemed to be incapable of understanding or expressing it clearly. And this, too me, appears to be the real reason why our relationship never became more than fun and games superficiality for me.

OTHER ENCOUNTERS

Being divorced wasn't at all how I had visualized it. Freedom, the singles game, parties, good looking women, that sort of thing. Unfortunately when we separated, I was running a small business out of my garage, had no close personal friends, didn't belong to any clubs or organizations, didn't know which bars to go to to meet the kind of people I might be interested in and was left with what seemed to be the only resource at the time. This was a singles register you could get for a dollar out of a news stand which was a fairly thick weekly publication with lots of names and box numbers to respond to.

I don't remember exactly what the first woman I made contact with claimed to be but I was interested and asked her out to dinner. And, not knowing anything about the area where she lived, I asked her to pick the restaurant. A nice place, it was relatively expensive. She asked for a glass of wine. Not the house wine but a particular label, perhaps to impress me with her good taste. We talked a little, me very new at the whole process. Then she ordered a second wine and an appetizer for herself, took about two bites of what she had gotten, asked the waiter for a box and set it aside. The same with the entree and an additional side dish.

Then she wanted a monstrous piece of pie for dessert, most of which also went in a box and by the time I got her out of the place, she had enough leftovers to sustain her for at least a week. Of course I was offended. The woman was dressed well enough, a little odd perhaps, a little withholding but not stupid so when I walked her to the door and she invited me in, I was curious. It was an apartment in an older building that looked in need of maintenance. And then, once inside, I understood her situation a lot better. The living room walls were painted a dark, dismal, green and the only furniture was a small couch and a coffee table and it was as far as I chose to go because a feeling of depressing gloom descended on me and almost literally forced me back out the door. And while it was an expensive lesson for me, I considered it to be my charitable act for the week and moved on.

The second woman I queried claimed to be a writer and a poet so I drove over to Santa Monica to meet her. Having learned something from my first experience, it was for lunch instead of dinner and that part of it was reasonable. As for the rest of it, talk about abusing editorial license, her writers background turned out to be nothing more than two terrible poems she had written, both of which she brought along and read to me. It was a short lunch to be sure.

As for number three, being much more cautious now, I made an after-work date for drinks only and would wait to see what happened. After one drink this, also claimed to be a writer, woman felt bold enough to read me the one and only short story she had ever written. I tried to listen politely enough and then ordered a second round, thinking that even though she would never make it as an author, maybe she had something else going for her. Having done that, I excused myself and went to the men's room. Then, returning to our table, I had no more than sat down when a group of four waiters appeared.

One of them was carrying a small cupcake with a lit candle on it. I looked at them, then looked at my date. She was smiling. The mini cake was placed in front of me and the waiters all began to sing happy birthday. What the hell? My birthday was still six months away and how would she have known that anyway? And then, after it was over, what did she do but laugh loudly and tell me she wanted to see if I had a sense of humor before things went any farther between us. They went further, all right. I finished my second drink, thanked her for an interesting time and was out the door.

Many months later, much more confident and experienced in the ways of the single world, thinking I now knew how to play the game, I met this very attractive blond in a Beverly Hills bar. We talked and ended by her saying I could take her to breakfast on Sunday. She would meet me in the restaurant of a particular hotel, a place I knew nothing about and with nothing else implied but food. Well, Sunday finally came and there she was, almost gorgeous and waiting in a very upscale place.

It wasn't a simple breakfast either. It was a, no prices on the menu, champagne brunch, the implication being that if you had to ask, you were probably in the wrong place. And, well enough, she ate what she ordered, nothing extra to take home in a box, drank her half of the bottle of champagne and we had a reasonable conversation. Then she asked me if I would give her a ride downtown to a woman's boutique she ran and drop her off. Of course I would. Why wouldn't I. Breakfast had only cost me about fifteen times more than it would have if we had gone to the coffee shop down the street instead, so why not throw in a little taxi service along with it.

The valet then brought up my car, held the door for her and off we went for about two blocks when she asked me to detour so she could run by her apartment on the way. No problem at all, I assured her and once there she asked if I'd like to see her place so I followed her in. It was very nice. Large, roomy, well furnished and then, as she pointed out, there on every wall in every room were fairly large framed pictures of her, the special part of which was that in every one she was totally nude, all in different poses. But not having been a subscriber, how was I know?

About ten years earlier this woman's pictures had been published in Playboy Magazine. She was the centerfold. October, I believe she said and with that we were back in the car and headed towards her place of business where she asked me for my phone number before getting out. It was only until later that I realized I didn't have hers but then, so what. After paying so much for our breakfast together I wasn't sure I would ever be able to afford taking her out to dinner, or any other place she might want to go. And besides, even though she was attractive and engaging enough, I also had to admit that there was little or nothing in the way of chemistry between us so I set the idea of pursuing her any further aside. But then, that done, I was surprised to have her call me about two weeks later. She was giving herself a birthday that Sunday afternoon and would I like to come. Same place where we had our brunch together.

I didn't know people did things like that. Give themselves birthday parties. Especially in an expensive place like that hotel where she had an open bar, drink all you wanted, it was on her. Plus lots of great hors d'oeuvres and live music to dance to for the approximately thirty guests that showed up. Surrounded by other people she was talking to when I arrived, she gave me a little wave and a smile but that was it so I went to the bar, got a drink and walked around, trying to see if there was anyone else there that I actually knew or at least someone who might be interested in some casual conversation. There was.

A woman who I didn't really know but recognized from somewhere who also recognized me and said hello. But then, no sooner than I had started to talk to her Miss Playboy tapped me on the shoulder. Leading me away, she took me back across the room to meet someone else. It was her, older than me, mother. Okay, I knew how to be polite, so we talked a little until she took me by the hand and asked me to dance. That was okay too, but once out on the floor she danced in close and began asking me questions about myself, some of which were on the more personal side. I thanked her after the music stopped and, having done my duty, was going to move on but she still had a solid grip on my hand, didn't seem ready to let go and pulled me back out onto the dance floor.

This time she put her arm around me, pulled in and snuggled up really close. Close enough so that all the contours of her figure were more more than apparent when we danced. Something which was enhanced by the way she moved her hips and rubbed her belly against mine. Then, as we circled the floor, I got a glimpse of her daughter, Miss Bunny, watching us, seeming to be quite pleased with the situation. So, was that what this was all about? I didn't like particularly like the conclusion I came to but what else could it be? Maybe mommy was even picking up the tab for the party. Certainly something was amiss.

Besides that there were very few men at the party and as far as I could tell the daughter basically ignored most of them during the time I had been there. Finally, that dance over I asked mommy if she needed another drink, because I certainly did. She accepted but when I returned she took one long sip and sat it down, saying she wanted to dance some more. Now feeling basically helpless, I took two very long slugs of my drink and reluctantly nodded my head in agreement, thinking I was prepared.

Not only was this dance as equally intimate as the last, it was bordering on obscenity. And now, not only was she was making little noises to go along with the rest of it, she was also nibbling on my ear as she did so. My god, I wondered. What would she do if I bent down and kissed her on the neck? Would she start shedding her clothes right there on the dance floor or would she begin groping me below the belt? But, already a bit embarrassed, I wasn't ready to try and find out. Also fortunate was the fact that I had to go to the men's room. At least that's what I told her, already aware that the men's room was down the hall near the front door. And finally, driving home alone, I assured myself once again that there is a place where good manners end and self preservation begins. But more than that it was also becoming very clear that if I was going to be any kind of player in the singles world I was now living in I would have to vastly improve my people reading skills in order to survive. As for meaningful encounters, in addition to those already described, there were others that had a good chance of developing into something more. Except they didn't.

For some people, coming home to an empty house is far worse than coming home to a troubled relationship and these are the ones who are often quite willing to settle for nothing more than a warm body to be around as they get older. Of course being alone can be difficult and I have known several people who immediately went from relationship to relationship to relationship, no time in between for some self searching. As a result they were never able to determine whether they hooking up with the wrong people or were they themselves, impossible to live with. Without that knowledge, things rarely get any better. So, bottom line I would have to agree with George Washington when he supposedly said that he would rather be alone than in bad company. Some other anonymous individual also said, "Better to love someone you can't have than have someone you can't love." Thus, for me, unless it is a question of absolute necessity and one is learning something from it, being with the wrong person is a mentally and emotionally destructive situation for both parties.

But who is to say. The last thing I wish to become is an expert on what is good for someone else. As for myself, there is just on last issue that I find to be important, relationship or not. it is the one about health. The last thing I ever want is to become a burden in my old age, either for my children or another person even though there might be such a person who would want nothing more than to be my caretaker. Even so, I would never want that burden imposed on myself at this point in life although I would honestly have to say that I still know of two women whose names will not be mentioned but who, if they showed up at my front door, I would probably let in to stay as long as they liked, no questions asked.

MEMORIES

Memories, memories, memories. In the end, what else is there that is of any real value even though, no matter how it all turns out, lingering questions still remain. What if? What if this, what if that, what if something else, an endless stream? How would it have played out then? Regardless, everything else taken into account as best it can be, I have only one serious regret. I wish that the mother of my children had stayed a little longer. Not only because I have continued to miss her but because of our children. Most definitely they would have been much better off with a mother to turn to along the way. The many times when she could have been there caring about them, loving them, giving support, enriching their lives, giving them things I was sometimes unable to do. And yes, if only I could have set my own needs aside at certain times and attended to theirs a little better.

Other than that life has been an interesting adventure, full of challenge, rewarded by some of the special people I have met and cared about along the way, far from over, I still have a lot to learn because life for me, has always been a search for meaning. There has always been that awareness that all too often I didn't know enough, didn't understand enough, lacked information and eventually came to realize that no matter how long a person lives, they never become a finished product but are always in a state of becoming instead. Some people keep evolving emotionally and intellectually right up to the end. Others stall out along the way, become rigid in their thinking and withdraw from life, something I tried never to do no matter how difficult things ever became.

Regardless, there were times when I felt trapped in life situations which I thought I had no control over. But, choice did exist and there were always options even though they sometimes seemed invisible and out of reach or the risk too great to make them worth going after. But living involves risks and living-more-fully involves overcoming fear and taking risks. I have known that, forgotten it and had to relearn it more than once. Additionally, I have also had to remind myself that my life also flowed more smoothly and ended up being more satisfying when I took the time to listen to my own inner voice instead of blindly accepting the opinions of life's gurus and other self appointed experts, especially about personal matters. And when I became ill along the way, there were reasons for it, most often grossly misunderstood, both by myself and the medical professionals. Reasons that ultimately come back to state of mind, belief systems and attitudes toward life in general.

Take my heart attack, for example. It was certainly not due to poor diet or lack of exercise but could well have been attributed to too much coffee and too much stress instead. Perhaps. But is it ever really that simple? Looking further, it could be said to have had it's beginnings in my emotional state at the time. Living with someone that on the one hand I cared about but at the same time never having felt so lonely in my life while being with her. In my opinion, it was a serious wake up call. I didn't die because I wasn't ready to die, close as I did come to it. And I didn't get well because I followed the doctor's advise. I got well because I never allowed myself to accept the idea of being limited physically. Or intellectually, psychologically or emotionally.

To see myself as weak and vulnerable would be, in my opinion, a mistake. Except for a few stitches due to an injury, I haven't been to a medical doctor, a healer or any other health expert in twenty seven years. I also don't have, don't want and don't feel the need for health insurance but may change my mind in another twenty years or so. And if I'm feeling okay mentally and physically, why would I want to go in for checkups and expose myself to all the negative possibilities about health that presently exist?

At the same time, however, I'm not saying that other people are wrong, just that this is an attitude that works for me. If someone else is convinced that they need medical guidelines to live by, then it is in their own best interest to follow them. As for the rest of the, how-one-should-live-their-life bits-of-wisdom, I have nothing to add. Challenge exists, the reward is in achieving the goals set, meeting new people and cherishing the special ones already there.

As for what is more important than what, that too, is entirely a personal thing. There was a period where I thought almost everything was of importance, then one where nothing was. And now, after all these years, I am of the opinion that some things are but most of the rest is not, something which becomes clearer as the days go by. Certainly there is some safety in conformity but if that is the only life goal a person has, they are probably going to end up feeling misled and disappointed when they get older.

And when it comes to the people I seek out and chose to let into my life, it is those who posses a certain degree of passion that I like the most. Not the loud, boisterous kind of reckless stupidity displayed by the few, nor the ego driven misfits who bulldoze their way through life trying to overcome their childhood insecurities, but the quieter ones who feel secure within themselves and follow their own inner voice. The ones you recognize when you look into their eyes and see that eternal bit of fire glowing in there, burning away with intensity. A bit of eccentricity and unconventionality is also always refreshing and can even include a certain amount of craziness at times. An alternate lifestyle is often interesting but bottom line it's the people who respect the lives of other people and other living things. The ones who can stand in the sun and feel blessed. Little house, big house, hut on the beach. Look at the sky and wonder. Feel the joy, feel the sadness, feel the pain. Stay a while, play a while, exchanging gifts along the way.